DON
GIOVANNI

MOZART'S

DON GIOVANNI

Libretto by
Lorenzo da Ponte

English translation
by
Amanda and Anthony Holden

ANDRE DEUTSCH

First published in this form in 1987 by Andre Deutsch Limited. 105–106 Great Russell Street, London WC1B 3LJ.

British Library Cataloguing in Publication Data

Mozart, Wolfgang Amadeus
  Mozart's Don Giovanni.
  1. Operas—Librettos
  I. Title II. Da Ponte, Lorenzo
  III. Holden, Anthony IV. Holden, Amanda
  V. Don Giovanni. *English*
  782.1'2   ML50.M939

  ISBN 0–233–98033–4

CONTENTS

ACKNOWLEDGEMENTS

We would like to thank Mark Elder, Jonathan Miller, Peter Robinson and Richard van Allan for the contributions they made to this translation.

INTRODUCTION

One summer day in 1985 we sat down in our London music room with Jonathan Miller, Mark Elder and a large pot of coffee, and embarked upon a long and vigorous discussion of Mozart's opera *Don Giovanni*. Three hours later we were formally commissioned to translate Lorenzo da Ponte's libretto into English for the new production they were mounting for English National Opera at the London Coliseum that autumn. The singers would need their parts at least two months before the start of rehearsals in October; so we were given just six weeks to deliver.

This was not quite as drastic as it sounds. We had already translated most of the first act in draft, and sketched out several arias in the second. Before the July deadline for our complete first version lay the prospect of long and fascinating days going through our work note by note with Jonathan and Mark (and later his deputy, Peter Robinson), scrutinising our text for faithfulness to both the spirit and the letter of Mozart/ da Ponte, and of course for its 'singability'. Beyond lay the process of attending rehearsals and solving any problems raised by the performers. We were both immensely enthused by the thought of a collaboration so detailed, so painstaking and so testing of our work.

Neither of us had translated an opera before. Amanda Holden is a pianist, a professor at the Guildhall School of Music, and a lifelong opera enthusiast. Anthony Holden is a writer and journalist with a deep but untutored love of music. In his youth he had undertaken several translations from the Greek: Pastoral Poetry for Penguin Classics, and a number of the ancient tragedies — one of which, *Agamemnon*, he converted into the libretto for a student opera performed in Oxford in 1969 (commissioned, as it happens, by one Amanda Warren – later Holden – and conducted by Peter Robinson). Another, *The Bacchae*, was lucky to last two weeks in 1972 as an off-Broadway rock musical entitled *Dionysus Wants You*. We had no obvious qualifications to translate an opera together beyond the facts that one of us was a musician, the other a wordsmith, and that we had been married for fourteen years.

Thanks, however, to years attending opera sung in English at the Coliseum, and to our friendship since university days with Mark Elder and David Pountney, now ENO's music director and director of productions, translating an opera was something we had long *thought* we could do. Because our professional lives had been entirely separate, the project held the further promise of being our first collaboration on anything beyond our three small sons. So it was a longstanding ambition, most recently raised in our home not long before, when Anthony, not for the first time, had somewhat unfairly demanded of Pountney just *when* ENO was going to offer us an opera to translate. 'It is not,' replied David firmly, 'as easy as you think.' He was to be proved absolutely right.

Pountney (who has himself translated many operas from several languages) suggested we discover just *how* difficult by 'having a crack' at *Là ci darem la mano*. Ten days later we found ourselves in unexpected retreat in a cottage in Dorset, stunned by a very sudden double bereavement. It proved a remarkable therapy each evening, once the children were tidied away, to sit at the piano together and work at this celebrated piece, the more fiendishly difficult to transpose into contemporary, rhyming English because of its familiarity to even the most occasional operagoer. We lay awake at nights with the music swimming around our heads, all sorts of versions tried and discarded. With so suggestive a duet of seduction and acceptance, it proved much easier to rhyme bawdy or vulgar lyrics than to polish elegant but accurate quatrains acceptable on the stage of a major opera house.

Là ci darem, in which Don Giovanni begins his vain attempts to seduce the peasant girl Zerlina on her wedding day, clarified the scale of the problems ahead. At the end of the preceding recitative, the Don has promised to marry Zerlina ('sposeremo'). The first two lines of the subsequent aria, which carry straight out of the recitative, are not merely, as in a literal translation, suggestive of sexual delight: 'There you will give me your hand, there you will say yes . . .'. In idiomatic Italian, the phrases suggest a wedding service: 'There we will plight our troth, there you will say "I do" . . .' Zerlina, though already on her way to her own wedding service to Masetto, seems surprisingly willing to accept, while the Don's proposal is of course pure humbug. How to reconcile these almost contradictory subtleties in da Ponte's text with the intensely romantic music lavished on them by Mozart?

Both librettist and composer, moreover, had suffused the development of the number with a highly charged sexuality, reaching a distinct anticipation of orgasm in Zerlina's eventual acceptance: 'Andiam'. How was this one climactic word, responding to itself in the form of a question from the Don, to be translated? Literally, as 'Let's go'? Too flat, too casual (though it fits the music adequately). That would suit the repeat at the end of the piece, as they sing the same word again together while skipping off to the Don's *casinetto*. What about 'You'll come? . . . I'll come'? More natural, giving the singers more scope for the appropriate innuendo – but the word 'come' in contemporary Anglo-Saxon has a double meaning which might raise a cheap laugh. Was it worth that risk?

Our instinctive aspiration was a clean-limbed, unobtrusive modern English text avoiding inversions, archaisms and other such bad habits which had had us cringing at other translations in the Coliseum stalls. At the same time it was a basic credo, put sternly to the test in these early sessions, to remain as faithful as possible to the Italian text – the letter of it where possible, the sense where not – and to reproduce da Ponte's complex, ubiquitous rhyme schemes (in a language, alas, much less easy to rhyme). Sometimes a contrived rhyme sounded so arch that we abandoned it in favour of more colourful and elegant English. It was, however, a hard and fast rule that, as in the Italian, every recitative ended on a rhyming couplet, as both a full stop to the section and a springboard to the ensuing aria. The rhythmic stresses naturally had to follow those dictated by the music, and the choice of open vowel sounds – especially on high or sustained notes – had to be comfortably singable. Roget's Thesaurus and the Rhyming Dictionary were to be consulted only *in extremis*, and then only to pursue improvements on an acceptable solution, even though the task did at times seem rather like solving a giant, multi-dimensional crossword puzzle.

Other, previous translations were of course available for consultation, but again we decided to do so only when we had worked out our own solution to a particular problem. Often other versions are merely distracting; when, as is only natural, you occasionally reach the same conclusion as a predecessor, there follows a nagging, quite unnecessary sense of guilt, or the feeling that you must find a different version just for the sake of it. Just occasionally there is a direct translation, a natural English idiom, which happens to fit both text and music, and it is hardly surprising if two translators both decide to adopt it.

But there were a surprising number of lines to which we found a literal English solution, where previous translators had all resorted to unnecessary periphrasis. In the closing scene of the first act, for instance, when the Don is again trying to lure Zerlina offstage, it is not difficult to have Anna, Elvira and Ottavio sing 'Just watch the villain tighten the noose around his neck' for 'L'iniquo da se stesso nel laccio se ne va'. But Edward J. Dent has 'Ah, now for his iniquity the man of sin shall pay!' and W. H. Auden and Chester Kallman, even more disappointingly, 'Now soon the vile intriguer will be exposed as vile!' Similarly, 'Gli vo' cavare il cor', the central line of Elvira's opening aria ('Ah! chi mi dice mai') emerges both comfortably and powerfully as 'Then I'll tear out his heart', where Dent has 'I'll make him pay the cost' and Auden-Kallman (with, perhaps, a touch of the magpie) 'And make him bear the scorn / That I alone have borne!', which later becomes 'You'll bear what I have borne'.

This last is a shining example of another temptation we resolved to avoid: providing different, often rhyming translations for repeated Italian lines. Though it is appealing in English to advance the sense of the text while scoring an easy rhyme or two, it seemed to us a fundamental betrayal of the translator's trust. It is a constituent element of Mozart's art to single out sundry da Ponte lines for repetition, for heightened emphasis but above all as an opportunity to develop musical characterisation. To mirror this in the text is to deny the music its function. In doing so, too many translators (notably Auden and Kallman) accord the words a significance they cannot bear in comparison with the music. One of the very few times we did, however, succumb to this temptation was for the sake of a – we hope – justified laugh, in sympathy with the wit of the music: in Leporello's 'catalogue' aria, for Mozart's repeat of da Ponte's 'e la grande maestosa', we couldn't resist mirroring Mozart's rising scale with 'If she's buxom, he won't fail her / Like a mountain he will scale her!'

In response to urgings from Mark Elder, we also aspired as far as possible to reflect the syntactical structure of the Italian. Clearly, in so different a language, so few of whose words end in feminine vowel sounds, this was not easy. But we believed it an important aspect of our respect for the primacy of the music to follow the Italian phrasing through musical rests or intervals. To take another example from the catalogue aria, it is all too tempting because of the musical phrasing to break into separate English phrases the Italian 'Nella bionda / egli ha l'usanza / di lodar / la gentilezza . . .' etc. We settled for 'If she's blonde-haired / his love grows stronger / ev'ry minute / he is beside her.' Yes, we have drifted somewhat from the strict meaning of the Italian, but we believed it justified in reflecting its sense, preserving the syntactical structure, and setting up the all-important rhymes on 'stronger' and 'beside her' ('he'll stay longer . . . woe betide her').

A hard taskmaster in these matters, Mark further urged us not to stray too far from the syllabic structure of the Italian on key words and notes, and above all at the end of lines. This proved a formidable challenge. Any English translator, we concluded, would be content simply to avoid strings of monosyllables where da Ponte has three- or four-syllable words. And there is an especial satisfaction when English can mirror some Italian alliteration, as in the last line of Elvira's recitative before 'Mi tradè', where 'Perchì questi sospiri . . .?' becomes in our version 'Ah, why this ceaseless sighing . . .?'

At least, as we cut our teeth on 'Là ci darem', there was a clear and famous example of how *not* to begin. The more familiar we became with E. J. Dent's 1921 translation of *Don Giovanni*, for so many years the standard one in performance, the more our respect grew for Dent's musicality, and for the role he played in bringing this and so many other great operas to English ears for the first time. But his famous opening to this duet is uncharacteristically dire; one friend misremembered it only slightly as 'You put your hand in mine, dear . . .' In fact it is 'You'll lay your hand in mine, dear . . .' ('lay' being another word to be used with caution in contemporary English, especially in this context). But Dent's failure to find a two-syllable solution to the end of the line, and thus the ensuing rhyme, was a salutary example of what to avoid. Because of Dent's notorious 'dear', we resolved wherever possible to shun such 'filler' words, notably 'now', 'then', 'Sir' etc, unless they were justified by the Italian text.

'Là ci darem' was, we knew, the moment at which the entire audience would be straining their ears: a stern test of a new translation. How many, we wondered, would know that in the original the first syllable of the first two lines placed great emphasis on the word 'there' – referring to the nearby *casinetto* to which the Don proposes to escort Zerlina? We went through several different versions – nicknamed 'bridal', 'romantic' and 'lustful' – before finding a way to combine all three elements. We resolved to place the notion of hand-holding, and that of not having far to go, in the end of the introductory recitative – which, as with the closing couplets of all recitatives, had to be rhymed à la da Ponte. This won us some freedom of movement in the opening couplet to combine a purely romantic lyricism with the overtones of a wedding service, setting up a couple of rhymes which, dare we say it, somewhat strengthened the Italian – departing from the literal meaning, but reflecting the mood of the moment. Thus, after 'I have a little house not far from here. We'll be alone there; I'll take your hand in mine, and make you my own there . . .', our version of 'Là ci darem' finally began:

There will my arms enfold you,
There you will say 'I do';
If you will let me hold you,
I'll make your dreams come true.

Dent's version is:

You'll lay your hand in mine, dear,
Softly you'll whisper 'Yes',
'Tis not so far to go, dear,
Your heart is mine, confess.

And Auden-Kallman's:

Here with our hands entwining,
Let our designs agree;
Lingering here serves no one;
Why not walk on with me?

The end of the duet provides one of the most fiendish examples of a trap Mozart and da Ponte regularly set for translators: an elision into one note of two vowel sounds originally accorded a note each. English can cope only when the sense lends itself to, for instance, 'Do not' becoming 'Don't', or 'You have' becoming 'You've' (viz, 'husband and father in me', as Don Ottavio tells Donna Anna) and so on. No such formula, however, fits the closing lines of 'Là ci darem', where Mozart also inverts da Ponte's original syntax, so that 'a ristorar le pene' becomes 'le pen(e) a ristorar [d'un innocente amor]'. All we could do here was modify our original 'Let's not delay the pleasure' to 'the pleasure soon we'll know [of innocent romance]'. This paid lip-service to the inversion (despite our distaste for the device in English), though we always felt it naggingly inadequate. In rehearsal it drifted further from the original, when the second 'pleasure', no longer needing to rhyme with 'treasure', was strengthened for musical reasons to 'rapture'.

We have dwelt on 'Là ci darem' in detail as a case-study in the minute problems of opera translation for the would-be purist. It is also an example of the inevitable smoothing-out, in opera house English, of the linguistic type-casting da Ponte employs for the different classes of character in his text. Where the Don is, of course, an aristocrat, Zerlina is a peasant; to expect them to use the same sophistication of language is again to stretch credibility for the sake of the music. We were always a little uneasy about this, having received a ruling on the subject from Mark Elder over our version of the opera's opening lines sung by Leporello:

Night and day I slave away,
Bad conditions, lousy pay,
Hungry, thirsty, short of sleep,
What a way to earn my keep!

'Lousy', decreed Mark, was just about as 'vulg' as we could get. At times, throughout the translation, we would rather have put bawdier or 'lower' language in the mouth, particularly, of Leporello, who bridges the worlds of the aristocrats and the peasants who people *Don Giovanni*. But it is one of the quirks of opera translation for a major house that the audience does not want to hear crude words as the vehicle for sublime music. Only in the recitatives, and in Masetto's one aria, 'Ho capito' (in our version, 'Oh, I get it'), did we manage to negotiate a little more leeway.

These strictures also applied, with even more difficulty, to the 'blue' jokes crowding the Italian text of the entire opera (which to its contemporary audience amounted to a pretty raunchy night out). Take, for instance, the *canzonetta* sung by the Don early in Act Two, beneath the window of Elvira's handmaid. It is pure pornography, suggesting between the Italian lines that unless she comes down at once, to help him relieve his throbbing pain, he will take matters, as it were, into his own hands. We aspired to our own contemporary brand of elegant innuendo, in the hope that the audience would perceive this number as more than merely a very pretty serenade. Elsewhere, especially when the Don and Leporello are busy about their *double entendres*, such words as 'upstanding' and 'satisfaction' were among the naughtiest acceptable contemporary English could manage.

It is one of the constant frustrations of opera translation that all too often the *mot* or phrase *juste* does unacceptable violence to the music. But obviously, as with prose and poetry, a translator encounters different problems when faced with recitative and aria. Where the recitative advances the action, the aria provides a pause for thought – not unlike the 'freeze-frame' in a movie or strip cartoon. And given that the arias are sacrosanct, we did discover a little room for manoeuvre in some of the recitatives.

The recitative is closer to natural speech rhythms, and accompanied harmonically by a keyboard, or occasionally set against a more colourful instrumental background (as in Donna Anna's accompanied recitative 'Don Ottavio, son morta' on p. 70). Though we made every effort to match our every English syllable to Mozart's notes in the recitatives, we found it justifiable at times to make very small adjustments to the rhythm of the voice part; a quaver might become two semiquavers, or two quavers on the same note might be tied, simply to adjust the speech rhythms from Italian to English. We always worked scrupulously within the framework of Mozart's harmony and melodic lines. Except in one minor and unavoidable instance (see note on 'I drink to women, I drink to wine', page 180), not one hair of Mozart's head did we touch.

Detailed explanations of these and other decisions we took may be found in the notes at the back of this book, signalled by superior numerals in the text, and restricted largely to explaining why the English may appear at moments to drift away from a strict rendering of the Italian. Suffice it to say here, in conclusion, a few words about some of the central characters, and the extent to which we tried to accord them their own vernacular.

The most difficult individual to bring to life in English was indubitably Donna Anna, not least because she is perhaps the most impenetrable character in the piece. What is the true nature of her relationship with Don Ottavio, and indeed of her feelings for Don Giovanni? Boredom with the first, and lust for the second, seem to be the immediate answers. But her outbursts are coloured with tones of disillusion and self-disgust which go much deeper. Whatever happened immediately before the action opens, when the Don penetrated her inner sanctum, left her feeling violated, polluted, whether or not Giovanni in fact had his way with her. She is 'affianced' to Ottavio, a fact which explains the strict protocol with which he behaves towards her, with a rulebook formality almost reminiscent of the mediaeval manners of courtly love. But she is obsessed with Giovanni, her horror that he should kill her father merely adding, of course, to her passion for him. With Jonathan Miller's encouragement, we heightened the atmospherics of the accompanied recitative in which she so dramatically describes the events of that fateful night; otherwise, we tried to give her a very worldly vocabulary, the more starkly to contrast her really rather basic, self-obsessed complaints with the more moving religious fervour of Donna Elvira.

Jonathan approached Elvira via the seventeenth-century *Letters of a Portuguese Nun*, and urged us to do likewise. Hers has been a very different betrayal from Anna's; before the action opens, we learn, the Don had promised to marry her (a regular ploy of his, it seems), seduced her, then after three days done a midnight flit. Not just Elvira herself, but vows she regards as sacred, have been violated. Yet the worse he treats her, the more hopelessly she loves him, as she makes evident in 'Mi tradi'. Her understandable efforts to conquer love with logic, in her balcony aria 'Ah taci, ingiusto core' ('Ah, why this raging fever?'), inspire Mozart to some of the most moving moments in the entire piece. Even her utter humiliation at the hands of the disguised Leporello – the Don at work by proxy – serves only to increase her tragic confusion. At the end, where Anna and Ottavio are permitted a highly protracted farewell to the audience, Mozart limits Elvira to one abrupt final line, a vow of withdrawal from the world.

As our work on the opera drew towards its end, we had left ourselves only those arias which had proved the toughest nuts to crack. Intriguingly, it emerged that the music which had proved most elusive was that of the Don himself. Though the opera's central character, he has only three short arias; the three women and Leporello get a much better deal. But from each of Giovanni's arias emerges a separate facet of his character. The first, the mysteriously nicknamed 'champagne' aria 'Fin ch'han dal vino', in which he looks forward to seducing the girls at that evening's party, portrays him as reckless, selfish and brash. (It is also, as is perfectly in character, fiendishly difficult to sing.) As we have already noted, the Act II canzonetta is a piece all but pornographic; it has been suggested that Mozart wrote in the *ritornelli* for the accompanying mandolin obbligato to allow room for the audience's laughter at its string of explicit sexual innuendoes. Here we hear the artful seducer at work, the lyrical beauty of his music in direct proportion to his total insincerity. Giovanni's last and most extended aria is 'Meta di voi . . .' Still disguised as Leporello, he sends Masetto's companions away to search for himself, so that he can beat Masetto up. The soft, insinuating nature of the music shows the Don at his craftiest, the repeated line at its close relishing the ease with which he has gulled the peasant into clearing the stage for his own undoing. The marked difference of his three arias, and the fact that there is little or no consistency about the Don's music, seemed to us perhaps Mozart's way of reflecting the emptiness of his soul. Accordingly, there was no particular need for consistency in the tone of his language, beyond a certain aristocratic disdain: he would always use whatever words suited his immediate purpose.

Ottavio, Jonathan ruled, was a lawyer, a decent but weak man unprepared to accept the case against the Don – despite the fact that his beloved is the chief prosecution witness – until presented with irrefutable evidence. Hence he doubts Anna's word after she first identifies Giovanni (a member, as it were, of his club) as the man who killed her father, and remains unconvinced until the unmasking of Leporello. Only then does he declare himself satisfied, and sets off to report the matter to the authorities ('Il mio tesoro').

The one difference of opinion we had with Mark Elder during the genesis of the production was over his decision to omit the other aria belonging to Don Ottavio in the 1788 Vienna version of *Don Giovanni*, 'Dalla sua pace'. Maldwyn Davies, who sang the role until Arthur Davies succeeded him, naturally agreed, as did the noted Mozartian Jane Glover, who pronounced over dinner one evening: 'To perform *Don Giovanni* without "Dalla sua pace" is like performing the Messiah without "I Know That My Redeemer Liveth"'. But Mark, a stickler for historical authenticity, insisted on performing the text as in the original Prague version of 1787, though he did include Elvira's 'Mi tradi' – which, with 'Dalla sua pace', was written in for a Viennese Ottavio a year later. The audience's evident disappointment, argued Elder, was outweighed by the fact that 'Dalla sua pace' slowed up the action at a critical moment and gave a relatively minor character a disproportionate amount of time at centre-stage. So our translation of this one piece has, at the time of writing, yet to be put to the test onstage.

Finally to Leporello: the servant half in love with his master, yet constantly shrinking from the enormity of his misdeeds. In Richard van Allan, we were lucky to have a Leporello of vast experience, who had sung the role many times under many distinguished conductors; in his time, indeed, Richard has sung every male role in the piece (except, of course, Ottavio), including the Don himself at Covent Garden. In rehearsal, his insights into the entire piece were of great value to us. Several of Leporello's best lines in our final version – notably his 'list of women fallen in action' – are attributable directly to Richard. A cheery telephone call, to point out a line of ours with which he was having difficulty, would inevitably result in some major improvement.

Our attendance at rehearsals was one of the most enjoyable stages of our work, as life was at last breathed into our text by the voices of these extremely distinguished singers. There were times at which Josephine Barstow grew as exasperated as we had with Donna Anna; some searching sessions with Mark at the piano, and her celebrated voice testing suggestion after suggestion, led to the resolution of one or two very difficult recitatives, notably that before 'Non mi dir'. Lesley Garrett (Zerlina) and Mark Richardson (Masetto) luckily found little in need of revision, and Felicity Lott returned from a concert tour of Australia with our Elvira already contentedly learnt. The Don himself, William Shimell, had also mastered his part even before the memorable first sing-through in an attic room of the Coliseum, and was steadfastly – and very professionally – reluctant to countenance any major changes. As we made minor adjustments here and there, however, we felt very much as if we were entering into the spirit of Mozart's collaboration with da Ponte, who took nearby rooms in Prague before the première in 1787 and shouted messages to each other across the alleyway.

They would have approved, we felt, of a little licence we felt free to exercise at the opening of the final dinner scene, by modernising a couple of 'in jokes' inaccessible to twentieth-century audiences. They were lines which would anyway have been improvised by the original performers, to raise some comic relief before the entry of the Commendatore's statue; and Richard van Allan, who had to sing them, confirmed to our relief that he felt them in sympathy with that endearing tradition. No previous translator has offered much beyond the literal for Leporello's lines as he serves the Don his last dinner, to the accompaniment of an onstage chamber orchestra. As it plays a theme from Martin y Soler's operetta *Cosa Rara*, a contemporary favourite, Leporello cries: 'Bravi! "Cosa Rara"!'

DON GIOVANNI

Che ti par del bel concerto?
(What do you think of this fine concert?)

LEPORELLO

E conforme, e conforme al vostro merto.
(It is worthy of your station.)

Having discovered that da Ponte also wrote the libretto for Martin's otherwise forgotten piece, we converted this exchange to:

DON GIOVANNI

So you like this operetta?

LEPORELLO

The words are by da Ponte, but Mozart sets them better.

Soon after, the band strikes up a theme from Paisiello's 'Fra i due litiganti il terzo gode'. Leporello cries: 'Evvivano 'i litiganti!' We managed to raise a laugh with: 'That's still not as good as Mozart'.

We naturally hope that the reader of this translation might have a score at his or her elbow, to share with us the problems we encountered, and follow the reasoning behind our conclusions. Those who know the opera well will, we are sure, find themselves singing along in their heads, thus perceiving what we were about. As a literal translation of da Ponte, it is of course eccentric. As a performing version, for the English-speaking world, of one of the greatest of all operas, we very much hope it gives the reader as much pleasure as it still, we cannot deny, gives us.

And to those who tell us that, for all our efforts, Mozart still sounds better in Italian, we can only reply: *Sì, certo*.

This translation of *Don Giovanni* was first performed by the English National Opera at the London Coliseum on 4 December 1985. The cast was as follows:

Leporello	Richard van Allan
Donna Anna	Josephine Barstow
Don Giovanni	William Shimell
Commendatore	John Connell
Don Ottavio	Maldwyn Davies
Donna Elvira	Felicity Lott
Zerlina	Lesley Garrett
Masetto	Mark Richardson
Conductor	Mark Elder
Designer	Philip Prowse
Producer	Jonathan Miller

ATTO PRIMO

ACT ONE

SCENA I

[Giardino. Notte – Leporello con ferraiolo, passeggia davanti alla casa di Donna Anna.]

N. 1 Introduzione

LEPORELLO

Notte e giorno faticar
Per chi nulla sa gradir;
Piova e vento sopportar,
Mangiar male e mal dormir.
Voglio far il gentiluomo,
E non voglio più servir.
Oh che caro galantuomo!
Voi star dentro colla bella,
Ed io far la sentinella!
Ma mi par che venga gente;
Non mi voglio far sentir.

[Si ritira. Don Giovanni esce dal palazzo del Commendatore inseguito da Donna Anna; cerca coprirsi il viso, ed é avvolto in un lungo mantello.]

DONNA ANNA

Non sperar, se non m'uccidi,
Ch'io ti lasci fuggir mai.

DON GIOVANNI

Donna folle! indarno gridi!
Chi son io tu non saprai.

LEPORELLO

Che tumulto! Oh, ciel, che gridi!
Il padron in nuovi guai!

DONNA ANNA

Gente! Servi! Al traditore!

DON GIOVANNI

Taci, e trema al mio furore.

DONNA ANNA

Scellerato!

SCENE 1

[A garden at night. Leporello, in a cloak, pacing up and down in front of Donna Anna's house.]

No. 1 Introduction

LEPORELLO

Night and day I slave away,
Bad conditions, lousy pay;
Hungry, thirsty, short of sleep,
What a way to earn my keep!
No, I'd rather be the master,
Not a servant any more.
What a fine upstanding master!
He's in there with someone's daughter,
I'm out here to play night porter.
What was that? There's someone coming;
I must hide behind this door.[1]

[He hides. Enter Donna Anna and Don Giovanni, she clutching him by the arm, he trying to hide his face.]

DONNA ANNA

Do not hope, unless you kill me,
I will ever let you go.

DON GIOVANNI

Hold your tongue! Your screams are futile;
Who I am you'll never know.

LEPORELLO

What confusion! Oh God, she's crazy.
He's in trouble. We should go.

DONNA ANNA

Someone help me hold this traitor!

DON GIOVANNI

Quiet, or you'll regret it later.

DONNA ANNA

Such intrusion!

DON GIOVANNI
Sconsigliata!

LEPORELLO
Sta' a veder che il libertino
Mi farà precipitar.

DONNA ANNA
Come furia disperata
Ti saprò perseguitar.

DON GIOVANNI
Questa furia disperata
Mi vuol far precipitar.

[Donna Anna, sentendo la voce del padre, entra in casa.]

COMMENDATORE
Lasciala, indegno!
Battiti meco!

DON GIOVANNI
Va': non mi degno
Di pugnar teco.

COMMENDATORE
Così pretendi da me fuggir?

LEPORELLO
Potessi almeno di qua partir!

DON GIOVANNI
Misero!

COMMENDATORE
Battiti!

DON GIOVANNI
Misero, attendi, se vuoi morir.

[Don Giovanni e il Commendatore si battono.]

COMMENDATORE
Ah, soccorso! Son tradito!
L'assassino m'ha ferito,
E dal seno palpitante
Sento l'anima partir.

[Muore.]

DON GIOVANNI

Such delusion!

LEPORELLO

Ah, this latest misadventure
Is the final straw, I know.

DONNA ANNA

I'll pursue you like a Fury;
I will never let you go.

DON GIOVANNI

She pursues me like a Fury;
This may prove the fatal blow.

[As the Commendatore enters, Donna Anna exits.]

COMMENDATORE

Leave her, you scoundrel!
I'll see you dead, sir!

DON GIOVANNI

No, it's beneath me.
Go back to bed, sir!²

COMMENDATORE

You are a coward. Your end is nigh.

LEPORELLO

If I could only bid him goodbye.

DON GIOVANNI

Idiot!

COMMENDATORE

Fight with me.

DON GIOVANNI

Idiot! So be it. Prepare to die.

[They fight.]

COMMENDATORE

Ah, I'm wounded. He's betrayed me.
This assassin has destroyed me.
Ah, I fear that I am dying,
Ah, my life, it slips away.

[He dies.]

29

DON GIOVANNI

Ah! già cadde il sciagurato.
Affannosa e agonizzante,
Già dal seno palpitante,
Veggo l'anima partir.

LEPORELLO

Qual misfatto! qual eccesso!
Entro il sen, dallo spavento
Palpitar il cor mi sento.
Io non so che far, che dir.

SCENA II

Recitativo

DON GIOVANNI

Leporello, ove sei?

LEPORELLO

Son qui, per disgrazia. E voi?

DON GIOVANNI

Son qui.

LEPORELLO

Chi è morto, voi o il vecchio?

DON GIOVANNI

Che domanda da bestia! Il vecchio.

LEPORELLO

Bravo! Due imprese leggiadre:
Sforzar la figlia, ed ammazzar il padre.

DON GIOVANNI

L'ha voluto: suo danno.

LEPORELLO

Ma Donna'Anna, cosa ha voluto?

DON GIOVANNI

Taci, non mi seccar! Vien meco,
se non vuoi qualche cosa ancor tu.

DON GIOVANNI

Ah, the wretched fool has fallen.
With each breath his death grows nearer.
Now, in pain, I see he's dying.
Yes, his life, it slips away.

LEPORELLO

How disastrous! How appalling!
I can feel my heartbeat racing.
I'm so frightened that I don't know
What to do or what to say.

SCENE 2

Recitative

DON GIOVANNI

Leporello, where are you?

LEPORELLO

I'm here, but wish I wasn't. And you?

DON GIOVANNI

I'm here.

LEPORELLO

Who's dead? You? Or the old man?

DON GIOVANNI

What a damn stupid question! The old man.

LEPORELLO

Bravo! Tell me, which would you rather?
Assault the girl, or assassinate her father?

DON GIOVANNI

It was his fault. He asked for it.

LEPORELLO

And Donna Anna? Did she ask for it too?

DON GIOVANNI

Silence! What impudence! Come with me,
or the same thing will happen to you.

LEPORELLO

Non vo' nulla, signor: non parlo più.

[Partono.]

SCENA III

[Donna Anna, Don Ottavio, e servi con lumi]

DONNA ANNA

Ah! del padre in periglio in soccorso voliam.

DON OTTAVIO

Tutto il mio sangue verserò, se bisogna.
Ma dov'è il scellerato?

DONNA ANNA

In questo loco . . .

[Vede il cadavere.]

N. 2 Recitativo e duetto

Ma qual mai s'offre, o Dei,
Spettacolo funesto agli occhi miei!
Il padre! Padre mio! Mio caro padre!

DON OTTAVIO

Signore!

DONNA ANNA

Ah! l'assassino mel trucido . . . quel sangue . . . quella piaga
. . . quel volto . . . tinto e coperto dei color di morte . . . ei
non respira più. . . fredde ha le membra . . . padre mio, caro
padre, padre amato! Io manco . . . io moro.

DON OTTAVIO

Ah! soccorrete, amici, il mio tesoro. Cercatemi, recatemi
. . . qualche odor . . . qualche spirto . . . Ah! non tardate
. . . Donna Anna! sposa! amica! . . . Il duol estremo la
meschinella uccide!

LEPORELLO

I will follow, my Lord, without more ado.

[Exeunt.]

SCENE 3

[Enter Donna Anna and Don Ottavio, with servants carrying lights.]

DONNA ANNA

Come, my father's in danger. We must hurry to help.

DON OTTAVIO

Every drop of my blood is yours to defend him.
Tell me, where's this intruder?

DONNA ANNA

This is where I left him . . .

[She sees her father's corpse.]

No. 2 Recitative and Duet

Oh my God, what do I see?
What awful apparition lies there before me?
Oh father! Darling father! Oh my dear father!

DON OTTAVIO

Signore!

DONNA ANNA

Ah! That assassin has struck him down. He's bleeding . . .
he is wounded . . . his face too . . . look how it wears a
deathly white complexion. His breathing has stopped . . .
how cold his hands are . . . Oh my father, dearest father,
father beloved! I'm fainting . . . I'm dying.

[She swoons.]

DON OTTAVIO

Go, fetch a doctor quickly . . . for my beloved. Bring
smelling salts, and medicine . . . get some help . . . bring
some water . . . and you must hurry! Donna Anna . . .
darling . . . companion! Ah, how I fear she'll die here
beside her father!

DONNA ANNA

Ahi!

DON OTTAVIO

Già rinviene. Datele nuovo aiuti.

DONNA ANNA

Padre mio!

DON OTTAVIO

Celate, allontanate agli occhi suoi quell'oggetto d'orrore.
Anima mia, consolati. Fa' core.

DONNA ANNA

Fuggi, crudele, fuggi!
Lascia ch'io mora anch'io.
Ora ch'è morto, o Dio,
Chi a me la vita diè!

DON OTTAVIO

Senti, cor mio, deh senti:
Guardami un solo istante!
Ti parla il caro amante,
Che vive sol per te.

DONNA ANNA

Tu sei! Perdon, mio bene.
L'affanno mio, le pene.
Ah, il padre mio dov'è?

DON OTTAVIO

Il padre? Lascia, o cara,
La rimembranza amara:
Hai sposo e padre in me.

DONNA ANNA

Ah! Vendicar, se il puoi,
Giura quel sangue ognor!

DON OTTAVIO

Lo giuro! Lo giuro!
Lo giuro agl' occhi tuoi,
Lo giuro al nostro amor!

DONNA ANNA

Ah!

DON OTTAVIO

She's reviving. Help me to lift her gently.

DONNA ANNA

My poor father!

DON OTTAVIO

Conceal him! Remove this horrible reminder somewhere
out of her sight.
Oh, my beloved, be comforted. Find courage.

DONNA ANNA

Leave me, you heartless creature!
Leave me to die beside him.
How could you think to hide him?
The man who gave me life.

DON OTTAVIO

Listen, my dearest, oh listen!
One look and you'll discover:
It's I, your faithful lover,
Who lives for you alone.

DONNA ANNA

Ottavio! Forgive your Anna.
My grief had made me forget you.
My father – where is he?

DON OTTAVIO

Your father? Leave behind you
Sorrows that might remind you.
You have husband and father in me.

DONNA ANNA

Swear! Swear an oath before me
That you'll avenge his death.

DON OTTAVIO

I swear it! I swear it!
I swear it by your eyes.
I swear it upon our love.

DONNA ANNA e DON OTTAVIO
Che giuramento, o Dei!
Che barbaro momento!
Tra cento affetti e cento
Vammi ondeggiando il cor.

[Partono.]

SCENA IV

[Alba chiara. Don Giovanni, Leporello]

Recitativo

DON GIOVANNI
Orsù, spicciati presto. Cosa vuoi?

LEPORELLO
L'affar di cui si tratta è importante.

DON GIOVANNI
Lo credo.

LEPORELLO
È importantissimo.

DON GIOVANNI
Meglio ancora. Finiscila.

LEPORELLO
Giurate di non andar in collera.

DON GIOVANNI
Lo giuro sul mio onore, purchè non parli del Commendatore.

LEPORELLO
Siamo soli?

DON GIOVANNI
Lo vedi.

LEPORELLO
Nessun ci sente?

DONNA ANNA and DON OTTAVIO
    Oh God, what have we promised
    At this horrific moment?
    A hundred thousand passions
    Swirling within my heart.[3]

    [Exeunt.]

SCENE 4

[Enter Don Giovanni and Leporello. Dawn is breaking.]

Recitative

DON GIOVANNI
    Come on now, get a move on. What's the matter?

LEPORELLO
    Listen to me a moment. It's important.

DON GIOVANNI
    I'm listening.

LEPORELLO
    It's really vital.

DON GIOVANNI
    It had better be. Well, out with it.

LEPORELLO
    Please promise not to get too angry.

DON GIOVANNI
    You have my word of honour – unless you mention the
    Commendatore.

LEPORELLO
    Are we alone here?

DON GIOVANNI
    That's obvious.

LEPORELLO
    No one can hear us?

DON GIOVANNI

Via!

LEPORELLO

Vi posso dire tutto liberamente?

DON GIOVANNI

Sì!

LEPORELLO

Dunque quando è così, caro signor padrone, la vita che menate è da briccone.

DON GIOVANNI

Temerario, in tal guisa . . . !

LEPORELLO

E il giuramento?

DON GIOVANNI

Non so di giuramenti. Taci, o ch'io . . .

LEPORELLO

Non parlo più, non fiato, o padron mio.

DON GIOVANNI

Così saremo amici.
Or odi un poco. Sai tu perchè son qui?

LEPORELLO

Non ne so nulla. Ma essendo l'alba chiara, non sarebbe qualche nuova conquista? Io lo devo saper per porla in lista.

DON GIOVANNI

Va' là, che sei il grand'uom! Sappi ch'io sono innamorato d'una bella dama, e son certo che m'ama. La vidi, le parlai: meco al casino questa notte verrà . . . Zitto! Mi pare sentire odor di femmina.

LEPORELLO

Cospetto, che odorato perfetto!

DON GIOVANNI

All'aria mi par bella.

LEPORELLO

E che occhio, dico!

DON GIOVANNI

No!

LEPORELLO

Then you'll permit me to speak my mind to you freely?

DON GIOVANNI

Yes!

LEPORELLO

Well, then, I have to say, dear and respected master . . .
about the life you're leading. It's a disaster.

DON GIOVANNI

You go too far. How dare you?

LEPORELLO

Your word of honour?

DON GIOVANNI

What do you know of honour? Silence, before . . .

LEPORELLO

My lips are sealed. I won't say one word more.

DON GIOVANNI

In that case we'll be friends.
Now you hear *me* out. Do you know why I'm here?

LEPORELLO

No, I know nothing. But it will soon be sunrise, and a new
dawn must mean an amorous transaction. Give me her
name for my list of women fallen in action.

DON GIOVANNI

That's more the man I know! Yes, I will tell you: I am in
love this time with a real beauty, and she's longing for me. I
saw her, had a word, and she is coming to my villa tonight
. . . Quiet! I'm sure I smell woman round the corner!

LEPORELLO

Amazing! This man's nose misses nothing.

DON GIOVANNI

Something tells me she's a beauty.

LEPORELLO

And his eyes see round corners.[4]

39

DON GIOVANNI

Ritiriamoci un poco, e scopriamo terren.

LEPORELLO

Già prese foco!

[Si ritirano a destra. Donna Elvira entra in abito da viaggio.]

SCENA V

N. 3 Aria

DONNA ELVIRA

Ah, chi mi dice mai
Quel barbaro dov'è,
Che per mio scorno amai,
Che mi mancò di fè.
Ah, se ritrovo l'empio
E a me non torna ancor,
Vo'farne orrendo scempio,
Gli vo' cavare il cor.

DON GIOVANNI

Udisti?
Qualche bella dal vago abbandonata.
Poverina!
Cerchiam di consolare il suo tormento.

LEPORELLO

Così ne consolò mille e ottocento.

DON GIOVANNI

Signorina, signorina . . .

Recitativo

DONNA ELVIRA

Chi è là?

DON GIOVANNI

Stelle! che vedo?

DON GIOVANNI
Let us hide here a moment, and we'll see what we can.

LEPORELLO
There's no holding this man!

[They hide. Enter Donna Elvira, in travelling clothes.]

SCENE 5

No. 3 Aria

DONNA ELVIRA
Where can I find the traitor
Who took my love in vain?
I gave him my devotion,
He gave me back disdain.
When I at last confront him,
If he insists we part,
I'll see him die in torment,
Then I'll tear out his heart.

DON GIOVANNI
Do you hear that?
This poor darling, abandoned by her lover.
Oh poor darling, oh poor darling . . .
Consoling her would be a pleasant pastime . . .

LEPORELLO
It won't be for the first time, or the last time.

DON GIOVANNI
Signorina, signorina . . .

Recitative

DONNA ELVIRA
Who's there?

DON GIOVANNI
Heavens! Not that one!

LEPORELLO

O bella! Donna Elvira!

DONNA ELVIRA

Don Giovanni! Sei qui, mostro, fellon, nido d'inganni!

LEPORELLO *[sotto voce]*

Che titoli cruscanti! Manco male che lo conosce bene.

DON GIOVANNI

Via, cara Donna Elvira, calmate questa collera. Sentite, lasciatemi parlar.

DONNA ELVIRA

Cosa puoi dire, dopo azion sì nera? In casa mia entri furtivamente, a forza d'arte, di giuramenti e di lusinghe arrivi a sedurre il cor mio; m'innamori, o crudele, mi dichiari tua sposa, e poi, mancando della terra e del cielo al santo dritto, con enorme delitto dopo tre dì da Burgos t'allontani, m'abbandoni, mi fuggi, e mi lasci in preda al rimorso ed al pianto, per pena forse che t'amai cotanto!

LEPORELLO *[sotto voce]*

Pare un libro stampato!

DON GIOVANNI

Oh, in quanto a questo, ebbi le mie ragioni.
[a Leporello] È vero?

LEPORELLO

È vero, e che ragioni forti!

DONNA ELVIRA

E quali sono se non la tua perfidia, la leggerezza tua? Ma il giusto cielo volle ch'io ti trovassi, per far le sue, le mie vendette.

DON GIOVANNI

Eh via, siate più ragionevole! *[sotto voce]* Mi pone a cimento costei! Se non credete al labbro mio, credete a questo galantuomo.

LEPORELLO

Terrific! Donna Elvira!

DONNA ELVIRA

Don Giovanni? You here? Monster, betrayer! Evil deceiver!

LEPORELLO [aside]

Well, she knows all his nicknames. But, you see, they've been very well acquainted.

DON GIOVANNI

My dear Donna Elvira, now do please try to calm yourself. Just listen, and I can explain all . . .

DONNA ELVIRA

What can you say after your vile behaviour? You wormed your way into my house – so furtively you entered – and with your pleading, your bold entreaties, with your sighs and your caresses, you had your way and seduced me. From that moment I loved you, and you said we'd be married. But then, you traitor, defying every law of earth and heaven, forswearing our betrothal, after three days you slipped away from Burgos. You walked out, you abandoned me, left me desolate, weeping and broken-hearted. I was in love: is that why you departed?[5]

LEPORELLO [aside]

This is just like a novel.

DON GIOVANNI

As far as that goes, I had my private reasons.
[to Leporello] Did I not?

LEPORELLO

You did, sir. Very private reasons!

DONNA ELVIRA

And what would they be? Except more peccadilloes, more unscrupulous betrayals? But God will grant me justice: he led me here to see that you are justly punished.

DON GIOVANNI

Come, come, aren't you rather overdoing it? [aside] This woman is getting on my nerves. If you will not believe what I say, then let this honest man convince you.

LEPORELLO [*sotto voce*]
Salve il vero!

DON GIOVANNI
Via, dille un poco.

LEPORELLO
E cosa devo dirle?

DON GIOVANNI
Sì, sì, dille pur tutto.

[*Don Giovanni fugge.*]

DONNA ELVIRA
Ebben, fa presto.

LEPORELLO
Madama, veramente . . . in questo mondo, conciossa cosa quando fosse che il quadro non è tondo . . .

DONNA ELVIRA
Sciagurato! Cosi del mio dolor giuoco ti prendi? Ah! voi . . . [*verso Don Giovanni*] Stelle! L'iniquo fuggì! Misera me! Dove? In qual parte?

LEPORELLO
Eh, lasciate che vada. Egli non merta che di lui ci pensiate.

DONNA ELVIRA
Il scellerato m'ingannò, mi tradì . . .

LEPORELLO
Eh, consolatevi! Non siete voi, non foste, e non sarete nè la prima, nè l'ultima. Guardate questo non picciol libro è tutto pieno di nomi di sue belle: ogni villa, ogni borgo, ogni paese è testimon di sue donnesche imprese.

N. 4 Aria

Madamina, il catalogo è questo
Delle belle che amò il padron mio:
Un catalogo egli è che ho fatt'io:

LEPORELLO *[aside]*

> All lies, as usual!

DON GIOVANNI

> Go on, you tell her.

LEPORELLO

> Which version shall I give her?

DON GIOVANNI

> The truth. Yes, tell her everything.

> *[Exits discreetly.]*

DONNA ELVIRA

> All right, I'm waiting.

LEPORELLO

> Signora, to speak truly . . . I'm sure you know that . . . it's just that . . . in a wicked world like this . . . a square is not a circle.[6]

DONNA ELVIRA

> You're no better! You know I've been betrayed, and yet you mock me. I'll tell . . . *[Turns to where Don Giovanni was.]* Heavens! Where's your master gone? Left me again! Help me! Where's he hiding?

LEPORELLO

> Oh, let him go his own way. Don't waste your time on him. He's not worth all this bother.

DONNA ELVIRA

> But he deceived me, the seducer, he's to blame . . .

LEPORELLO

> Try not to think of it. You never were, nor are now, nor ever will be his first love or his last one. Look closely. This not so little book here overflows with all the women he's persuaded. Every village, every city and every nation bears ample witness to his determination.

No. 4 Aria

> Little lady, you are not going to like this.[7]
> It's a list of the loves of my master.
> Though to you it may prove a disaster,

Osservate, leggete con me.
In Italia seicento e quaranta;
In Almagna duecento e trentuna;
Cento in Francia, in Turchia novantuna;
Ma in Ispagna son già mille e tre.
V'han fra queste contadine,
Cameriere, cittadine,
V'han contesse, baronesse,
Marchesine, principesse,
E v'han donne
D'ogni grado, d'ogni forma, d'ogni età,
D'ogni forma, d'ogni età.

Nella bionda egli ha l'usanza
Di lodar la gentilezza,
Nella bruna la costanza,
Nella bianca la dolcezza.
Vuol d'inverno la grassotta,
Vuol d'estate la magrotta;
È la grande maestosa,
La piccina è ognor vezzosa.
Delle vecchie fa conquista
Pel piacer di porle in lista;
Sua passion predominante
È la giovin principiante.
Non si picca se sia ricca,
Se sia brutta, se sia bella;
Purchè porti la gonnella,
Voi sapete quel che fa.

[Parte.]

Pay attention, and listen to me.
First Italians, six hundred and forty;
Then the Germans two hundred and thirty;
A hundred in France, only ninety in Turkey;
But, but the Spanish! One thousand and three.
There are chambermaids a-plenty,
Country girls and city gentry,
Baronesses and countesses,
Marchionesses and princesses.
Here you see them:
Every age and every shape and every size,
Every shape and every size.

If she's blonde-haired, his love grows stronger
ev'ry moment he is beside her;[8]
If she's dark-haired, he'll stay longer.
If she's pale-skinned, woe betide her!
In the winter plump and tender,
In the summer oh so slender . . .
If she's buxom, he won't fail her;
Like a mountain he will scale her.[9]
If she's tiny, teeny-tiny,
He'll overwhelm her.
Even widows, shy about their ages,
Still swell numbers here in these pages.
But the highest common factor
Is the girl who's still intacta.
Rich or poor, or wife or whore,[10]
Or on the floor, behind a door,
He'll still perform if hidden by a curtain,
Just as long as she has a skirt on,
You'll be certain what he wants.

[Exit.]

47

SCENA VI

Recitativo

DONNA ELVIRA

In questa forma dunque mi tradì il scellerato. È questo il premio che quel barbaro rende all'amor mio? Ah, vendicar vogl'io l'ingannato mio cor; pria ch'ei mi fugga si ricorra, si vada, io sento in petto sol vendetta parlar, rabbia e dispetto!

[Parte.]

SCENA VII

[Masetto, Zerlina e coro di contadini e contadine]

N. 5 Duetto e Coro

ZERLINA

Giovinette che fate all'amore,
Non lasciate che passi l'età.
Se nel seno vi bulica il core,
Il rimedio vedetelo qua.
Ah, che piacer che sarà!

CONTADINE

Ah, che piacer che sarà, tralalerala!

MASETTO

Giovinetti leggieri di testa,
Non andate girando di là.
Poco dura de' matti la festa,
Ma per me comminciato non ha.
Ah, che piacer che sarà!

CONTADINI

Ah, che piacer che sarà, tralalerala!

ZERLINA e MASETTO

Vieni, carino, godiamo,
E cantiamo e balliamo e saltiamo!
Che piacer che sarà.

SCENE 6

Recitative

DONNA ELVIRA

So that is his true nature, the wretch who deceived me. I'm
left with nothing to repay my undying devotion. I'll have
revenge upon him for my suffering heart. He won't escape
me. I will stalk him; I'll hound him. He'll make confession.
Righteous wrath be my spur, vengeance my obsession!

[Exit.]

SCENE 7

[Zerlina and Masetto, with a chorus of peasants]

No. 5 Duet and Chorus

ZERLINA

All you girls who can't wait for a lover,
Don't you fritter your best years away.
If it's pleasure you want to discover,
Find a husband without more delay.
Ah, I am going to be married today!

WOMEN'S CHORUS

Ah, she is going to be married today, tralalerala!

MASETTO

All you men should love one woman only,
Never let your eye wander astray, this way, that way.
While a bachelor's life is so lonely,
Married bliss is one long holiday.
Ah, I am going to be married today!

MEN'S CHORUS

Ah, he is going to be married today, tralalerala!

ZERLINA and MASETTO

We'll have dancing and drinking and singing,
To the sound of our wedding bells ringing,
For we're going to be married today.

SCENA VIII

[Don Giovanni e Leporello]

Recitativo

DON GIOVANNI
Manco male, è partita. Oh guarda, che bella gioventù; che belle donne!

LEPORELLO
Fra tante, per mia fè, vi sarà qualche cosa anche per me.

DON GIOVANNI
Cari amici, buon giorno. Seguitate a stare allegramente, seguitate a suonar, o buona gente. C'è qualche sposalizio?

ZERLINA
Sì, signore, e la sposa son io.

DON GIOVANNI
Me ne consolo. Lo sposo?

MASETTO
Io, per servirla.

DON GIOVANNI
Oh bravo! Per servirmi; questo è vero parlar da galantuomo.

LEPORELLO *[a parte]*
Basta che sia marito!

ZERLINA
Oh, il mio Masetto è un uom d'ottimo core.

DON GIOVANNI
Oh anch'io, vedete! Voglio che siamo amici. Il vostro nome?

ZERLINA
Zerlina.

DON GIOVANNI
E il tuo?

SCENE 8

[Enter Don Giovanni and Leporello.]

Recitative

DON GIOVANNI

Thank God we've seen the back of her. Oh, look there, just look! What very pretty girls! What lovely women!

LEPORELLO

Perhaps, you never know, there might be a few who'd fancy me.

DON GIOVANNI

Friends, I bid you good morning! Won't you tell me what you are celebrating? Carry on: I don't want to interrupt you. Is someone getting married?

ZERLINA

Yes, your lordship. It is I who's the bride.

DON GIOVANNI

I've missed my chance, then! And the bridegroom?

MASETTO

Me. At your service.

DON GIOVANNI

Oh, bravo! At my service. I'm a man who appreciates good manners.

LEPORELLO *[aside]*

He appreciates the bride too!

ZERLINA

Oh, my Masetto was very well brought up, sir.

DON GIOVANNI

Ah, just like me then! We ought to get acquainted. What is your name, dear?

ZERLINA

Zerlina.

DON GIOVANNI

And yours is . . . ?

MASETTO

Masetto.

DON GIOVANNI

O caro il mio Masetto! Cara la mia Zerlina! V'esibisco la mia protezione.

[a Leporello che fa dei scherzi alle altre contadine]

Leporello! Cosa fai lì, birbone?

LEPORELLO

Anch'io, caro padrone, esibisco la mia protezione.

DON GIOVANNI

Presto, va' con costor: nel mio palazzo conducili sul fatto. Ordina ch'abbiano cioccolatta, caffè, vini, prosciutti. Cerca divertir tutti, mostra loro il giardino, la galleria, le camere; in effetto fa' che resti contento il mio Masetto. Hai capito?

LEPORELLO

Ho capito. Andiam.

MASETTO

Signore!

DON GIOVANNI

Cosa c'è?

MASETTO

La Zerlina senza me non può star.

LEPORELLO

In vostro loco vi sarà sua eccellenza; e saprà bene fare le vostre parti.

DON GIOVANNI

Oh, la Zerlina è in man d'un cavalier. Va pur, fra poco ella meco verrà.

ZERLINA

Va', non temere. Nelle mani son io d'un cavaliere.

MASETTO

Masetto.

DON GIOVANNI

Now listen, dear Masetto, and you, my dear Zerlina, I would like to offer you all possible assistance.

[to Leporello, who is flirting with the girls]

Leporello . . . what do you think you're doing?

LEPORELLO

I'm following your example. Just like you, I am offering assistance.

DON GIOVANNI

Right, then, here is your chance. Why don't you take all our friends here to my villa, make sure there's plenty for them to eat there. Serve wine, lay on a banquet. Give them the run of the gardens, show them round all the bedrooms. Make them at home there. Yes, everywhere. What I really want you to do is entertain Masetto. Have you got that?

LEPORELLO

Yes, I've got it. Let's go.

MASETTO

One moment.

DON GIOVANNI

What is it now?

MASETTO

My Zerlina cannot stay here without me.[11]

LEPORELLO

But you can leave her in the care of my master. You can be sure she'll be very well looked after.

DON GIOVANNI

Yes, your Zerlina will be quite safe with me. You go, we'll join you all there in a while.

ZERLINA

Go, don't you worry. In the hands of a gentleman, I'm safe.

MASETTO

E per questo?

ZERLINA

E per questo non c'è da dubitar.

MASETTO

Ed io, cospetto!

DON GIOVANNI

Olà, finiam le dispute. Se subito senz' altro replicar non te ne vai, Masetto, guarda ben, ti pentirai!

N. 6 Aria

MASETTO

Ho capito, signor sì.
Chino il capo e me ne vo.
Giacchè piace a voi così,
Altre repliche non fo.
Cavalier voi siete già.
Dubitar non posso affè;
Me lo dice la bontà
Che volete aver per me.

[a Zerlina, a parte]

Bricconaccia, malandrina!
Fosti ognor la mia ruina.

[a Leporello]

Vengo, vengo.

[a Zerlina]

Resta, resta.
È una cosa molto onesta!
Faccia il nostro cavaliere
Cavaliera ancora te.

[Masetto parte con Leporello ed i contadini.]

MASETTO

That's what you think.

ZERLINA

That's what I think: you've no cause for concern.

MASETTO

So I'm not wanted!

DON GIOVANNI

Come, come, do stop this bickering. If you don't hurry up and go away, you will upset me. Masetto, you'll regret you ever met me.

No. 6 Aria

MASETTO

Oh, I get it. Yes, I see.
Bow my head and off I go.
You don't want the likes of me:
What you really want I know.
Just because you are a Don,
Just because you are Your Grace,
Say the word and I am gone,
Oh yes, sir, I know my place.

[aside, to Zerlina]

Little trollop! I could kill you!
Make a cuckold of me, will you?

[to Leporello]

Yes, I'm coming.

[to Zerlina]

I'll go drinking.[12]
Ah, I know what you are thinking.
You just want to let our master
Make a mistress out of you.

[Exit, with Leporello and the Chorus.]

SCENA IX

Recitativo

DON GIOVANNI

Alfin siam liberati, Zerlinetta gentil, da quel scioccone. Che ne dite, mio ben, so far pulito?

ZERLINA

Signore, è mio marito.

DON GIOVANNI

Chi? Colui? Vi par che un onest'uomo, un nobil cavalier, come io mi vanto, possa soffrir che quel visetto d'oro, quel viso inzuccherato da un bifolcaccio vil sia strapazzato?

ZERLINA

Ma, signor, io gli diedi parola di sposarlo.

DON GIOVANNI

Tal parola non vale un zero. Voi non siete fatta per esser paesana; un altra sorte vi procuran quegli occhi bricconcelli, quei labbretti sì belli, quelle dituccie candide e odorose, parmi toccar giuncata e fiutar rose.

ZERLINA

Ah, non vorrei . . .

DON GIOVANNI

Che non vorreste?

ZERLINA

Alfine ingannata restar. Io so che raro colle donne voi altri cavalieri siete onesti e sinceri.

DON GIOVANNI

Eh, un impostura della gente plebea! La nobiltà ha dipinta negli occhi l'onestà. Orsù, non perdiam tempo; in questo istante io vi voglio sposar.

SCENE 9

Recitative

DON GIOVANNI

At last we're rid of him, Zerlinetta my sweet. He's just a peasant. Don't you think, little one, I saw him off well?

ZERLINA

But sir, he's to be my husband.

DON GIOVANNI

What, him? Do you think a man of honour, a gentleman like me, of noble breeding, could stand and watch while someone of your beauty, a woman quite so alluring, could throw herself away on such a yokel?

ZERLINA

But, kind sir, I have already said that I would marry him.

DON GIOVANNI

My dear child, such a vow means nothing. You were never meant to be an ordinary housewife. I'll change your fortunes, if you'll let me admire these eyes that sparkle; and these lips are for kissing, these lovely little fingers for caressing, these pretty hands for holding. They smell of roses.[13]

ZERLINA

Ah, but I cannot . . .

DON GIOVANNI

You cannot what?

ZERLINA

I cannot risk your breaking my heart. I have been warned to stay away from all gentlemen of your kind, who never keep their promises.

DON GIOVANNI

That is a slander, put about in the back streets. I am a man you can trust. Can't you see it in my eyes? Come on, we're wasting time here. At this very moment, I would make you my wife.

ZERLINA

Voi?

DON GIOVANNI

Certo, io. Quel casinetto è mio. Soli saremo, e là, gioiello
mio, ci sposeremo.

N. 7 Duettino

DON GIOVANNI

Là ci darem la mano,
Là mi dirai di si.
Vedi, non è lontano,
Partiam, mio ben, da qui.

ZERLINA

Vorrei e non vorrei,
Mi trema un poco il cor.
Felice, è ver, sarei,
Ma può burlarmi ancor.

DON GIOVANNI

Vieni, mio bel diletto!

ZERLINA

Mi fà pietà Masetto!

DON GIOVANNI

Io cangerò tua sorte.

ZERLINA

Presto non son più forte.

DON GIOVANNI

Andiam!

ZERLINA

Andiam!

DON GIOVANNI e ZERLINA

Andiam, andiam, mio bene,
A ristorar le pene
D'un innocente amor.

ZERLINA

You?

DON GIOVANNI

Yes, of course me. I have a little house not far from here.
We'll be alone there. I'll take your hand in mine, and make
you my own there.

No. 7 Duettino[14]

DON GIOVANNI

There will my arms enfold you,
There you will say I do.
If you will let me hold you,
I'll make your dreams come true.

ZERLINA

I'd like to go, but should I?
My heart is filled with fear.
I'd be his wife, or would I?
He may prove insincere.

DON GIOVANNI

Darling, you must come with me!

ZERLINA

Masetto'd never forgive me!

DON GIOVANNI

You need be poor no longer!

ZERLINA

I wish that I were stronger.

DON GIOVANNI

You'll come!

ZERLINA

I'll come.

DON GIOVANNI and ZERLINA

Let's go, let's go, my treasure,
Let's not delay the pleasure
Of innocent romance.

Andiam, andiam, mio bene,
Le pene a ristorar
D'un innocente amor.

[S'incamminano abbracciati verso il casino]

SCENA X

Recitativo

DONNA ELVIRA

Fermati, scellerato! Il ciel mi fece udir le tue perfidie. Io sono a tempo di salvar questa misera innocente dal tuo barbaro artiglio.

ZERLINA

Meschina! Cosa sento?

DON GIOVANNI

[A parte] Amor, consiglio!

[A Donna Elvira]

Idol mio, non vedete ch'io voglio divertimi?

DONNA ELVIRA

Divertirti? È vero! Divertirti! Io so, crudele, come tu ti diverti.

ZERLINA

Ma, signor cavaliere, è ver quel ch'ella dice?

DON GIOVANNI

[a parte a Zerlina]

La povera infelice è di me innamorata, e per pietà deggio fingere amore, ch'io son, per mia disgrazia, uom di buon core.

N. 8 Aria

DONNA ELVIRA

Ah, fuggi il traditor!
Non lo lasciar più dir.

Let's go, my love, let's go,
The rapture soon we'll know
Of innocent romance.

[They set off arm in arm towards Don Giovanni's house.]

SCENE 10

Recitative

DONNA ELVIRA

Leave her alone, you monster! God willed that I arrive to overhear you. I'm just in time to rescue this innocent young maiden from your barbarous clutches.

ZERLINA

Who is this? What's she saying?

DON GIOVANNI

[aside] Oh, Venus help me!

[to Donna Elvira]

My dear heart, can't you see I'm only being friendly?

DONNA ELVIRA

Being friendly? Oh yes? Being friendly? I know, you demon, just what you mean by friendship.

ZERLINA

But you're a gentleman, sir. Can all she says be true?

DON GIOVANNI

[aside, to Zerlina]

This poor distracted woman is quite hopelessly in love with me, and so I'm forced to pretend I adore her. I'm much too tender-hearted to ignore her.

No. 8 Aria

DONNA ELVIRA

Escape the traitor's arms,
He means to do you wrong.

Il labbro è mentitor,
Fallace il ciglio.
Da' miei tormenti impara
A creder a quel cor,
E nasca il tuo timor
Dal mio periglio.

[Parte, conducendo seco Zerlina.]

SCENA XI

Recitativo

DON GIOVANNI

Mi par ch'oggi il demonio si diverta d'opporsi a' miei
piacevoli progressi; vanno mal tutti quanti.

[Entrano Don Ottavio e Donna Anna.]

DON OTTAVIO

Ah! Ch'ora, idolo mio, son vani i pianti, di vendetta si parli.
Ah, Don Giovanni!

DON GIOVANNI [a parte]
Mancava questo intoppo!

DONNA ANNA

Signore, a tempo vi ritroviam. Avete core? Avete anima
generosa?

DON GIOVANNI

[a parte] Sta' a vedere che il diavolo gli ha detto qualche
cosa.

[a Donna Anna] Che domanda! Perchè?

DONNA ANNA

Bisogno abbiamo della vostra amicizia.

DON GIOVANNI

[a parte] Mi torna il fiato in corpo.

[a Donna Anna] Comandate. I congiunti, i parenti, questa

Beware his fatal charms,
For he'll betray you.
The wrongs that I have suffered
Should not be yours to share.
Beware, my child, beware,
He will betray you.

[Exit, taking Zerlina with her]

SCENE 11

Recitative

DON GIOVANNI

It seems the devil's out to make some mischief, and seizes
every chance to thwart my plans. I will rise to his
challenge.

[Enter Don Ottavio and Donna Anna.]

DON OTTAVIO

I beg of you, dear heart, you must stop weeping. We are
here to seek vengeance. Ah, Don Giovanni!

DON GIOVANNI *[aside]*
This clown is all I needed![15]

DONNA ANNA

Signore, our paths have crossed just in time. Are you
courageous? Have you a generous heart and soul?

DON GIOVANNI

[aside] Now we'll see if the devil has been whispering in
her ear!

[to Donna Anna] What a question! What's wrong?

DONNA ANNA

We need your friendship, and we need your assistance.

DON GIOVANNI

[aside] That was a nasty moment . . .

[to Donna Anna] At your service. All my kinsmen, and my

man, questa ferro, i beni, il sangue spenderò per servirvi. Ma voi, bella Donna Anna, perche così piangete? Il crudele chi fu che osò la calma turbar del viver vostro?

[Entra Donna Elvira.]

SCENA XII

DONNA ELVIRA
Ah! ti ritrovo ancor, perfido mostro!

N. 9 Quartetto

Non ti fidar, o misera,
Di quel ribaldo cor!
Me già tradì quel barbaro,
Te vuol tradir ancor.

DONNA ANNA e DON OTTAVIO
Cieli, che aspetto nobile,
Che dolce maestà!
Il suo pallor, le lagrime
M'empiono di pieta.

DON GIOVANNI
[a parte; Donna Elvira ascolta]

La povera ragazza
È pazza, amici miei;
Lasciatemi con lei,
Forse si calmerà.

DONNA ELVIRA
Ah non credete al perfido!

DON GIOVANNI
È pazza, non badate!

DONNA ELVIRA
Restate, o dei, restate!

household, this my arm and my weapon . . . my power . . .
I would spend all for your satisfaction.[16] But say, lovely
Donna Anna, what is it so upsets you? Who has done you
such wrong? What man has dared to disrupt your life so
cruelly?

[Enter Donna Elvira.]

SCENE 12

DONNA ELVIRA
   Ah, must it always be so, heartless deceiver!

No. 9 Quartet

   Don't ever put your trust in him;
   He is the worst of men.
   He has deceived me shamelessly,
   And he'll deceive again.

DONNA ANNA and DON OTTAVIO
   Heavens! She has such dignity!
   What sweet and noble bearing!
   Her tearful eyes, her heavy sighs
   Move me to pity her.

DON GIOVANNI
   *[to Donna Anna and Don Ottavio, but Donna Elvira
   overhears him]*

   This poor distracted female
   Is crazy, friends, she's crazy.
   Please go and leave her with me,
   Leave me to calm her down.

DONNA ELVIRA
   Ah, don't believe this hypocrite!

DON GIOVANNI
   She's crazy. Take no notice.

DONNA ELVIRA
   Please stay. Don't leave me here with him.

DONNA ANNA e DON OTTAVIO
A chi si crederà?

DONNA ANNA e DON OTTAVIO
Certo moto d'ignoto tormento
Dentro l'alma girare mi sento.
Che mi dice, per quell'infelice,
Cento cose che intender non sa.

DON GIOVANNI
Certo moto d'ignoto tormento
Dentro l'alma girare mi sento.
Che mi dice, per quell'infelice,
Cento cose che intender non sa.

DONNA ELVIRA
Sdegno, rabbia, dispetto, tormento
Dentro l'alma girare mi sento,
Che mi dice, di quel traditore,
Cento cose che intender non sa.

DON OTTAVIO [a parte]
Io di quà non vado via
Se non scopro questo affar.

DONNA ANNA [a parte]
Non ha l'aria di pazzia
Il suo tratto, il suo parlar.

DON GIOVANNI
Se men vado, si potria
Qualche cosa sospettar.

DONNA ELVIRA
Da quel ceffo si dovria
La ner' alma giudicar.

DON OTTAVIO [a Don Giovanni]
Dunque quella . . .

DON GIOVANNI
È pazzarella.

DONNA ANNA [a Donna Elvira]
Dunque quegli . . .

DONNA ANNA and DON OTTAVIO
>What are we to believe?

DONNA ANNA and DON OTTAVIO
>She so rouses my fear and suspicion
>That we'll force him to make an admission.
>Someone's wronged her, and she's trying to tell us:
>What has happened I don't yet perceive.

DON GIOVANNI
>She so rouses their fear and suspicion
>That they'll force me to make an admission.
>Someone's wronged her, and she's trying to tell them:
>What has happened they don't yet perceive.

DONNA ELVIRA
>He so rouses my scorn and derision
>that I'll force him to make a confession.
>I've been wronged by this sinful seducer:
>What has happened they don't yet perceive.

DON OTTAVIO [aside]
>I'm determined not to leave here
>While this matter is in doubt.

DONNA ANNA [aside]
>Judging by this lady's manner,
>She's sound-minded and devout.

DON GIOVANNI
>They're suspicious. If I leave them,
>They will surely find me out.

DONNA ELVIRA
>His malevolent expression
>Shows his soul is black throughout.

DON OTTAVIO [to Don Giovanni]
>So you're saying . . .

DON GIOVANNI
>She's gone quite crazy.

DONNA ANNA [to Donna Elvira]
>And you're saying . . .

DONNA ELVIRA
È un traditore.

DON GIOVANNI
Infelice!

DONNA ELVIRA
Mentitore!

DONNA ANNA e DON OTTAVIO
Incomincio a dubitar.

DON GIOVANNI [sotto voce a Donna Elvira]
Zitto, zitto, che la gente
Si raduna a noi d'intorno;
Siate un poco più prudente,
Vi farete criticar.

DONNA ELVIRA [a Don Giovanni]
Non sperarlo, o scellerato,
Ho perduta la prudenza;
Le tue colpe ed il mio stato
Voglio a tutti palesar.

[Parte.]

DONNA ANNA e DON OTTAVIO [a parte]
Quegli accenti sì sommessi,
Quel cangiarsi di colore,
Son indizi troppo espressi
Che mi fan determinar.

Recitativo

DON GIOVANNI
Povera sventurata! I passi suoi voglio seguir; non voglio che
faccia un precipizio. Perdonate, bellissima Donna Anna; se
servirvi poss'io, in mia casa v'aspetto. Amici, addio.

[Parte.]

DONNA ELVIRA
>This man is evil.

DON GIOVANNI
>Poor young woman!

DONNA ELVIRA
>You're a liar!

DONNA ANNA and DON OTTAVIO
>I begin to have my doubts.

DON GIOVANNI *[quietly, to Donna Elvira]*
>Do be quiet. They are listening.
>You must pull yourself together.
>Say much more and there'll be gossip.
>It will quickly get about.

DONNA ELVIRA *[to Don Giovanni]*
>There's no hope for you, seducer.
>I don't care what they are thinking.
>You have wronged me and deceived me,
>And the world must know the truth.

>*[Exit.]*

DONNA ANNA and DON OTTAVIO *[aside]*
>Why this whisp'ring? He looks guilty.
>You can see he's hiding something.
>From the way he treats this lady,
>We must ask her for the proof.

Recitative

DON GIOVANNI
>Poor little senseless creature! I'd better follow and take her in hand. In this mood she may do something foolish. Please excuse me, most beautiful Donna Anna. If I can be of service, you know just where to find me. My friends, I'll leave you.

>*[Exit.]*

SCENA XIII

N. 10 Recitativo e Aria

DONNA ANNA

Don Ottavio, son morta!

DON OTTAVIO

Cosa è stato?

DONNA ANNA

Per pietà, soccorretemi!

DON OTTAVIO

Mio bene, fate coraggio!

DONNA ANNA

O dei!
Quegli è il carnefice del padre mio!

DON OTTAVIO

Che dite?

DONNA ANNA

Non dubitate più. Gli ultimi accenti che l'empio proferì, tutta la voce richiamar nel cor mio di quell' indegno che nel mio appartamento . . .

DON OTTAVIO

O ciel! Possibile che sotto il sacro manto d'amicizia . . . ma come fu? Narratemi lo strano avvenimento.

DONNA ANNA

Era già alquanto avanzata la notte, quando nelle mie stanze, ove soletta mi trovai per sventura, entrar io vidi, in un mantello avvolto, un uom che al primo istante avea preso per voi. Ma riconobbi poi che un inganno era il mio.

DON OTTAVIO

Stelle! Seguite!

DONNA ANNA

Tacito a me s'appressa e mi vuole abbracciar; sciogliermi cerco, ei più mi stringe; io grido; non viene alcun! Con una

SCENE 13

No. 10 Recitative and Aria

DONNA ANNA

Don Ottavio: I'm dying!

DON OTTAVIO

What's the matter?

DONNA ANNA

If you love me, then rescue me!

DON OTTAVIO

My darling, how can I help you?

DONNA ANNA

I know now![17]
He is the murderer of my dear father.

DON OTTAVIO

What can you mean . . . ?

DONNA ANNA

Now there can be no doubt. The way he spoke just now, the way he took his leave, everything about him, brings rushing back that awful night when in my bedroom . . .

DON OTTAVIO

Oh no! I can't believe that under the sacred guise of friendship . . . But tell me more. What really happened on that dreadful evening?

DONNA ANNA

Dawn was approaching. The house was still in darkness, and I was asleep in my room when something suddenly woke me. There was someone standing by my bedside . . . a dark and silent shadow . . . at first I thought it might be you. But all too soon I realised that I was mistaken.

DON OTTAVIO

Heavens! Continue.

DONNA ANNA

Silently he approaches me, and he wants to embrace me. I try to escape, but he holds me tightly. I cry out, but no one mano cerca d'impedire la voce, e coll' altra m'afferra stretta così, che già mi credo vinta.

DON OTTAVIO
Perfido! E alfin?

DONNA ANNA
Alfine il duol, l'orrore dell'infame attentato accrebbe sì la lena mia, che a forza di svincolarmi, torcermi e piegarmi, da lui mi sciolsi!

DON OTTAVIO
Ohimè! Respiro!

DONNA ANNA
Allora rinforzo i stridi miei, chiamo soccorso; fugge il fellon; arditamente il seguo fin nella strada per fermarlo, e sono assalitrice d'assalita. Il padre v'accorre, vuol conoscerlo, e l'iniquo, che del povero vecchio era più forte, compie il misfatto suo col dargli morte!

Or sai chi l'onore
Rapire a me volse,
Chi fu il traditore
Che il padre mi tolse.
Vendetta ti chiedo,
La chiede il tuo cor.
Rammenta la piaga
Del misero seno,
Rimira di sangue
Coperto il terreno,
Se l'ira in te langue
D'un giusto furor.

[Parte.]

comes. With one hand, he tries to stop me from screaming, with the other he grips me so very tight I think that I am ruined.[18]

DON OTTAVIO

Horrible. And then . . . ?

DONNA ANNA

And then the fear, the horror of his evil intentions, at last gives me strength to fight him. By twisting and turning desperately, hitting him, even biting . . . thus I escape him.

DON OTTAVIO

Oh God, I thank you!

DONNA ANNA

So now I cry again for help . . . louder and louder. In panic he runs. I quickly chase him as far as the street, to catch him. So now I am pursuing my pursuer. My father runs out, comes to rescue me. And the stranger, who is stronger by far when challenged to duel, proves himself the very devil, proves himself the very devil, with murder most cruel.

You know who assaulted
Both father and daughter.
My honour he threatened,
My father he slaughtered.
If you truly love me,
Your heart must seek revenge,
Remember my father
Defending me bravely,
Remember the bloodshed
He suffered to save me.
His memory is sacred,
He must be avenged.

[Exit.]

SCENA XIV

Recitativo

DON OTTAVIO

Come mai creder deggio, di sì nero delitto capace un cavaliero! Ah, di scoprire il vero ogni mezzo si cerchi. Io sento in petto e di sposo e d'amico il dover che mi parla: disingannarla voglio, o vendicarla.

N. 10a Aria

Dalla sua pace
La mia dipende;
Quel che a lei piace
Vita mi rende,
Quel che le incresce
Morte mi dà.
S'ella sospira,
Sospiro anch'io;
È mia quell'ira,
Quel pianto è mio;
E non ho bene,
S'ella non l'ha.

[Exit.]

SCENA XV

Recitativo

LEPORELLO

Io deggio ad ogni patto per sempre abbandonar questo bel matto. Eccolo qui; guardate con qual indifferenza se ne viene.

DON GIOVANNI

Oh, Leporello mio, va tutto bene?

LEPORELLO

Don Giovannino mio, va tutto male.

SCENE 14

Recitative

DON OTTAVIO

How can I believe that such a cold-blooded murder was committed by a gentleman? Ah, I must seek the truth; I shall not rest till I know it. It is my duty as a lover and a friend to pursue a solution. Either I prove her wrong, or seek retribution.

No. 10a Aria

Her cares are my cares,
Her pain is my pain;
While she is suff'ring
I live in vain.
Whatever hurts her
Puts me to death.
When she is sighing,
Her sighs are my sighs;
And when she's crying,
Her tears fill my eyes.
I'll seek to cheer her
With my last breath.[19]

[Exit.]

SCENE 15

Recitative

LEPORELLO

This can't go on much longer. I've got to find a way to leave this madman. Ah, here he comes. Just look there. You'd never guess that he was in such trouble!

DON GIOVANNI

Everything's going splendidly, my Leporello!

LEPORELLO

Everything's going badly, my Don Giovanni.

DON GIOVANNI

Come va tutto male?

LEPORELLO

Vado a casa, come voi l'ordinaste, con tutta quella gente.

DON GIOVANNI

Bravo!

LEPORELLO

A forza di chiacchere, di vezzi e di bugie, ch'ho imparato si bene a star con voi, cerco d'intrattenerli.

DON GIOVANNI

Bravo!

LEPORELLO

Dico mille cose a Masetto per placarlo, per trargli dal pensier la gelosia.

DON GIOVANNI

Bravo, in coscienza mia!

LEPORELLO

Faccio che bevano e gli uomini e le donne. Son già mezzo ubbriacchi. Altri canta, altri scherza, altri seguita a ber. In sul più bello, chi credete che capiti?

DON GIOVANNI

Zerlina.

LEPORELLO

Bravo! E con lei chi viene?

DON GIOVANNI

Donna Elvira.

LEPORELLO

Bravo! E disse di voi . . .

DON GIOVANNI

Tutto quel mal che in bocca le venia.

LEPORELLO

Bravo, bravo, in coscienza mia.

DON GIOVANNI

What do you mean? Going badly?

LEPORELLO

I took them home, sir, and did all you told me, for the whole wedding party . . .[20]

DON GIOVANNI

Bravo!

LEPORELLO

I chattered away to them, I lied to them as usual, using all the tricks I've learnt from you. That's how I kept them happy . . .

DON GIOVANNI

Bravo!

LEPORELLO

I was very careful to occupy Masetto, to keep his mind off any jealous brooding . . .

DON GIOVANNI

Bravo! Upon my conscience!

LEPORELLO

I made sure they drank a lot, the men as much as the women. They were already tipsy; some were singing; some were giggling; some did nothing but drink. And in the middle of it, who do you think chose to turn up?

DON GIOVANNI

Zerlina.

LEPORELLO

Bravo! And guess who was with her?

DON GIOVANNI

Donna Elvira.

LEPORELLO

Bravo! And said about you . . .

DON GIOVANNI

Everything nasty her tiny mind could think of.

LEPORELLO

Bravo! Upon my conscience!

DON GIOVANNI
E tu, cosa facesti?

LEPORELLO
Tacqui.

DON GIOVANNI
Ed ella?

LEPORELLO
Seguì a gridar.

DON GIOVANNI
E tu?

LEPORELLO
Quando mi parve che già fosse sfogata, dolcemente fuor dell'orto la trassi, e con bell'arte chiuso la porta a chiave io mi cavai, e sulla via soletta la lasciai.

DON GIOVANNI
Bravo, bravo, arcibravo! L'affar non può andar meglio. Incominciasti, io saprò terminar. Troppo mi premono queste contadinotte; le voglio divertir finchè vien notte.

N. 11 Aria

DON GIOVANNI
Fin ch'han dal vino
Calda la testa,
Una gran festa
Fa' preparar.
Se trovi in piazza
Qualche ragazza,
Teco ancor quella
Cerca menar.
Senza alcun ordine
La danza sia;
Chi'l minuetto,
Chi la follia,
Chi l'alemanna
Farai ballar.
Ed io frattanto

DON GIOVANNI

And what was your reaction?

LEPORELLO

Silence.

DON GIOVANNI

And Elvira?

LEPORELLO

She carried on.

DON GIOVANNI

And you?

LEPORELLO

When I thought she'd got it all off her chest, very gently I
led her through the door, and rather neatly managed to
lock her out, while I slipped back inside, and left her all
alone out in the street.

DON GIOVANNI

Bravo! Bravo! That was brilliant! It couldn't be better.
You've got things started, and I'll finish them off. These
lovely country girls are making me excited; if I can have my
way, I'll be delighted.

No. 11 Aria

DON GIOVANNI

Now that the wine has
Stopped them from thinking
Let's have more drinking,
Women and song.
If on the way there
You see some girls spare,
See that they're all mine,
Bring them along.
Bring ev'ry girl you meet,
Get them all dancing,
First a flamenco,
Then a follia,
Then a bolero,
Dance every one.[21]
While they are kissing

Dall'altro canto
Con questa e quella
Vo' amoreggiar.
Ah, la mia lista
Doman mattina
D'una decina
Devi aumentar!

SCENA XVI

[Giardino con due porte chiuse per di fuori. Coro di contadini e contadine, sparse qua e là, che dormono e siedono sopra sofa d'erbe]

Recitativo

ZERLINA

Masetto, senti un pò'; Masetto, dico.

MASETTO

Non mi toccar.

ZERLINA

Perchè?

MASETTO

Perchè mi chiedi? Perfida! Il tatto sopportar dovrei d'una man infedele?

ZERLINA

Ah no! taci, crudele, io non merto da te tal trattamento.

MASETTO

Come? Ed hai l'ardimento di scusarti? Star sola con un uom, abbandonarmi il dì delle mie nozze! Porre in fronte a un villano d'onore questa marca d'infamia! Ah, se non fosse lo scandalo, vorrei . . .

ZERLINA

Ma se colpa io non ho, ma se da lui ingannata rimasi; e poi, che temi? Tranquillati, mia vita; non mi toccò la punta

They won't be missing
This one and that one,
I'll have some fun.
And by the morning
There will be plenty,
I'll give you twenty
Names for the list.

SCENE 16

[The garden of Don Giovanni's house. Locked gates. The chorus of peasants are slumped or asleep.]

Recitative

ZERLINA

Masetto, won't you listen? Masetto, listen!

MASETTO

You keep your hands off!

ZERLINA

And why?

MASETTO

What do you mean, why? Shameless slut! What makes you think that I should listen to a girl who's unfaithful?

ZERLINA

Oh no, don't be so cruel. I don't think I deserve that kind of treatment.

MASETTO

Don't you? You always have plenty of excuses! You went off with that man! Went off and left me standing at the altar, made a fool of me in front of everyone – me, an honest working man. Ah, if it wouldn't cause a scandal, I'd like to . . .

ZERLINA

What if I'm not to blame? What if he tried and wasn't successful? So why be nervous? Calm down, my love, don't worry. He didn't even touch the tips of my fingers.

81

delle dita. Non me lo credi? Ingrato! Vien qui, sfogati, ammazzami, fa tutto di me quel che ti piace; ma poi, Masetto mio, ma poi fa pace.

N. 12 Aria

ZERLINA

Batti, batti, o bel Masetto,
La tua povera Zerlina;
Starò qui come agnellina
Le tue botte ad aspettar.
Lascierò straziarmi il crine,
Lascierò cavarmi gli occhi,
E le care tue manine
Lieta poi saprò baciar.
Ah, lo vedo, non hai core!
Pace, pace, o vita mia,
In contenti ed allegria
Notte e dì vogliam passar.

Recitativo

MASETTO *[a parte]*

Guarda un po', come seppe questa strega sedurmi! Siamo pure i deboli di testa!

DON GIOVANNI *[di dentro]*

Sia preparato tutto a una gran festa.

ZERLINA

Ah, Masetto, Masetto, odi la voce del monsù cavaliero!

MASETTO

Ebben, che c'è?

ZERLINA

Verrà!

MASETTO

Lascia che venga.

ZERLINA

Ah, se vi fosse un buco da fuggir!

You don't believe me? That's not fair! Come here. Shout at me, do anything; hit me, if it helps you make amends. But then, Masetto dearest, let us be friends.

No. 12 Aria

ZERLINA

Beat me, beat me, my Masetto,
Beat your sorrowful Zerlina.
Here I'll stand, like a lamb,
I'll endure your every blow.
I will let you tear my hair out!
I will let you pluck my eyes out!
And I'll kiss the hands that beat me,
For my love is true, you know.
Ah, I see now, you are heartless!
Make it up, let's be united.
Both contented and delighted,
Night and day with you I'll spend.

Recitative

MASETTO *[aside]*

Little witch! How she twists me round her dear little finger! It is men who really are the weaker sex!

DON GIOVANNI *[from within]*

See everything is ready for a grand banquet!

ZERLINA

Ah, Masetto, Masetto, that was his lordship. That was his voice!

MASETTO

What if it was?

ZERLINA

He's coming.

MASETTO

Well, let him come, then.

ZERLINA

Ah, I must quickly find a place to hide.

MASETTO

Di cosa temi? Perchè diventi pallida? Ah, capisco, capisco, bricconcella! Hai timor ch'io comprenda com'è tra voi passata la faccenda.

N. 13 Finale

MASETTO

Presto, presto, pria ch'ei venga,
Por mi vo' da qualche lato;
C'è una nicchia qui celato,
Cheto, cheto mi vo' star.

ZERLINA

Senti, senti, dove vai?
Ah, non t'asconder, o Masetto!
Se ti trova, poveretto,
Tu non sai quel che può far.

MASETTO

Faccia, dica quel che vuole.

ZERLINA

Ah, non giovan le parole!

MASETTO

Parla forte, e qui t'arresta.

ZERLINA

Che capriccio ha nella testa?

MASETTO *[sotto voce]*

Capirò se m'è fedele,
E in qual modo andò l'affar.

[Entra nella nicchia.]

ZERLINA *[sotto voce]*

Quell'ingrato, quel crudele
Oggi vuol precipitar.

MASETTO

Why are you trembling? What has made you so
frightened? Ah, I see it. I see, you two-faced thing, you,
you're afraid I'll discover it is true you really were his lover.

No. 13 Finale

MASETTO

Quickly, quickly! He is coming!
I must hide where he can't see me.
Here's a corner. This will do me.
If I listen, he won't know.

ZERLINA

Listen, listen! Wait a minute!
You must not risk it, my Masetto.
If he finds you, you're in trouble,
You don't know what he might do.

MASETTO

I shall watch while you are wooing.

ZERLINA

Ah, you don't know what you're doing.

MASETTO

Don't you try to mend your fences!

ZERLINA

You have really lost your senses!

MASETTO [softly]

I'll find out what she's been up to,
What she's told him, and where she's been. [Hides]

ZERLINA [softly]

This is crazy. He is jealous.
He just wants to cause a scene.

SCENA XVII

DON GIOVANNI [con servi nobilmente vestiti]

[ai contadini e contadine]

Sù, svegliatevi: da bravi!
Sù, coraggio, o buona gente!
Vogliam stare allegramente,
Vogliam ridere e scherzar.

[ai servi]

Alla stanza della danza
Conducete tutti quanti,
Ed a tutti in abbondanza
Gran rinfreschi fate dar.

CORO DI SERVI
Sù, svegliatevi: da bravi!
Sù, coraggio, o buona gente!
Vogliam stare allegramente,
Vogliam ridere e scherzar.

[Partendo.]

SCENA XVIII

ZERLINA
Tra quest'arbori celata,
Si può dar che non vi veda.

DON GIOVANNI
Zerlinetta, mia garbata,
T'ho già visto, non scappar!

ZERLINA
Ah lasciatemi andar via!

DON GIOVANNI
No, no, resta, gioia mia!

ZERLINA
Se pietade avete in core . . .

SCENE 17

DON GIOVANNI *[entering, with liveried servants]*

[to chorus of peasants/guests]

Come along, my friends, look lively!
You should see the preparations:
It's a night for celebrations,
For enjoyment and goodwill!

[to servants]

Get them dancing, get them singing,
Let the house be filled with laughter,
Let me hear the rafters ringing,
Let them eat and drink their fill!

CHORUS OF SERVANTS

Come along, my friends, look lively!
You should see the preparations,
It's a night for celebrations,
For enjoyment and goodwill!

[Exeunt.]

SCENE 18

ZERLINA

I will hide around this corner
In the hope that he won't see me.

DON GIOVANNI

Zerlinetta, my beloved,
I can see you, I can see you, don't be shy.

ZERLINA

Let me go. I can't be seen here.

DON GIOVANNI

Who will know, my love, you've been here?

ZERLINA

Can it be you have no feeling?

DON GIOVANNI

Sì, ben mio, son tutto amore.
Vieni un poco in questo loco,
Fortunata io ti vo' far.

ZERLINA

Ah, s'ei vede il sposo mio,
So ben io quel che può far.

DON GIOVANNI *[vedendo Masetto]*

Masetto!

MASETTO

Sì, Masetto.

DON GIOVANNI

E chiuso là, perchè?
La bella tua Zerlina
Non può, la poverina,
Più star senza di te.

MASETTO

Capisco, sì signore.

DON GIOVANNI

Adesso fate core.
I suonatori udite?
Venite omai con me.

ZERLINA e MASETTO

Sì, sì, facciamo core,
Ed a ballar cogli altri
Andiamo tutti tre.

[Partono.]

SCENA XIX

[Donna Anna, Donna Elvira e Don Ottavio in maschera]

DONNA ELVIRA

Bisogna aver coraggio,
O cari amici miei,

DON GIOVANNI
    Yes I have, it needs your healing.
    Let me take you round this corner,
    We'll be lovers, you and I.

ZERLINA
    My Masetto, should he see us,
    He will kill us both this time.

DON GIOVANNI *[discovers Masetto]*
    Masetto!

MASETTO
    Yes, Masetto.

DON GIOVANNI
    And hiding there? You too?
    You fool! For while you hide here,
    Your lovely little bride here
    Is pining just for you.[22]

MASETTO
    Too true, my lord, oh yes, too true.

DON GIOVANNI
    Cheer up, let's join the dancing!
    Come on, I hear them playing,
    Let's all go arm in arm.

ZERLINA and MASETTO
    Yes, yes, let's join the dancing,
    It's time to join the others,
    Let's all go arm in arm.

    [Exeunt.]

SCENE 19

    [Enter Donna Anna, Donna Elvira, Don Ottavio, masked.]

DONNA ELVIRA
    Oh heaven, grant us courage.
    My friends, we must confront him,

E i suoi misfatti rei
Scoprir potremo allor.

DON OTTAVIO

L'amica dice bene,
Coraggio aver conviene;
Discaccia, o vita mia,
L'affanno ed il timor.

DONNA ANNA

Il passo è periglioso,
Può nascer qualche imbroglio.
Temo pel caro sposo,
E per noi temo ancor.

LEPORELLO *[fuori dalle finestre]*

Signor, guardate un poco,
Che maschere galanti!

DON GIOVANNI

Falle passar avanti,
Dì che ci fanno onor.

DONNA ANNA e DONNA ELVIRA e DON OTTAVIO

Al volto ed alla voce
Si scopre il traditore.

LEPORELLO

Zi, zi! Signore maschere! Zi, zi!

DONNA ANNA e DONNA ELVIRA *[a Don Ottavio piano]*

Via, rispondete.

LEPORELLO

Zi, zi! Signore maschere!

DON OTTAVIO

Cosa chiedete?

LEPORELLO

Al ballo, se vi piace,
V'invita il mio signor.

DON OTTAVIO

Grazie di tanto onore!
Andiam, compagne belle.

And all his evildoing
Make plain, make plain for all to see.

DON OTTAVIO

She's right, this is the moment
To face him and expose him.
Take heart now, my beloved,
And put your trust in me.

DONNA ANNA

Our path is fraught with danger,
Each step could prove our last one,
I fear for you, beloved,
I fear for us, all three.

LEPORELLO *[at a window]*

Sir, do you see what I see?
Three stylish masqueraders.

DON GIOVANNI

We must invite them in, then.
Tell them they're welcome here.

DONNA ANNA, DONNA ELVIRA and DON OTTAVIO

That face and that familiar voice
Betray the man we're after.

LEPORELLO

Psst, psst! You masqueraders! Psst, psst!

DONNA ANNA and DONNA ELVIRA *[to Don Ottavio, softly]*

Give him an answer.

LEPORELLO

Psst, psst! You masqueraders!

DON OTTAVIO

How can I help you?

LEPORELLO

We're dancing here, and feasting.
My lord invites you in.

DON OTTAVIO

Tell him we're deeply honoured.
This way, my dear companions.

LEPORELLO *[a parte, chiuda la fenestra]*
L'amico anche su quelle
Prove farà d'amor.

DONNA ANNA e DON OTTAVIO
Protegga il giusto cielo
Il zelo del mio cor!

DONNA ELVIRA
Vendichi il giusto cielo
Il mio tradito amor!

[Partono.]

SCENA XX

[Sala illuminata e preparata per una gran festa di ballo]

DON GIOVANNI *[a contadine]*
Riposate, vezzose ragazze.

LEPORELLO *[a contadini]*
Rinfrescatevi, bei giovinotti.

DON GIOVANNI e LEPORELLO
Tornerete a far presto le pazze.
Tornerete a scherzar e ballar.

DON GIOVANNI
Ehi! caffè!

[si portano i rinfreschi]

LEPORELLO
Cioccolata!

MASETTO
Ah, Zerlina, giudizio!

DON GIOVANNI
Sorbetti!

LEPORELLO
Confetti!

LEPORELLO *[aside, closing the window]*
    They won't be yours much longer.
    He's set his heart on sin.[23]

DONNA ANNA and DON OTTAVIO
    Protect, O God of justice,
    Protect my zealous heart.

DONNA ELVIRA
    Vengeance, O God of justice,
    Avenge my broken heart.

    [Exeunt.]

SCENE 20

[A brilliantly lit hall, prepared for feasting and dancing]

DON GIOVANNI *[to a group of girls]*
    Won't you stay here beside me a moment?

LEPORELLO *[to their men]*
    Come with me, there is plenty of wine left.

DON GIOVANNI and LEPORELLO
    Yet alas we can't keep you apart long;
    You will want to get back to the dance.

DON GIOVANNI
    Petits fours!

[refreshments are brought in]

LEPORELLO
    Have another!

MASETTO
    Now, Zerlina, be careful!

DON GIOVANNI
    A sorbet!

LEPORELLO
    Another?

ZERLINA e MASETTO *[a parte]*
  Troppo dolce comincia la scena;
  In amaro potria terminar.

DON GIOVANNI *[fa carezze a Zerlina]*
  Sei pur vaga, brillante Zerlina.

ZERLINA
  Sua bontà.

MASETTO *[incollerito]*
  La briccona fa festa.

LEPORELLO *[imita il padrone colle altre ragazze]*
  Sei pur cara, Giannotta, Sandrina!

MASETTO
  Tocca pur, che ti cada la testa!

ZERLINA *[a parte]*
  Quel Masetto mi par stralunato,
  Brutto, brutto si fa quest'affar.

DON GIOVANNI e LEPORELLO
  Quel Masetto mi par stralunato.
  Qui bisogna cervello adoprar.

MASETTO
  Tocca, tocca! Ah, briccona!
  Ah, briccona, mi vuoi disperar!

  *[Entrano Donna Anna, Donna Elvira e Don Ottavio,
  mascherati.]*

LEPORELLO
  Venite pur avanti,
  Vezzose mascherette!

DON GIOVANNI
  È aperto a tutti quanti,
  Viva la libertà!

DONNA ANNA, DONNA ELVIRA e DON OTTAVIO
  Siam grati a tanti segni
  Di generosità.

TUTTI
  Viva la libertà!

ZERLINA and MASETTO *[aside]*

> Ah, the night has begun much too smoothly;
> There'll be trouble before it is through.

DON GIOVANNI *[fondling Zerlina]*

> You're the belle of the ball, my Zerlina.

ZERLINA

> You're too kind!

MASETTO *[furious]*

> She's the belle of the ball, eh?

LEPORELLO *[imitating Don Giovanni]*

> You're the belle of the ball, my Sandrina!

MASETTO

> If he touches her I'll knock his block off.

ZERLINA *[aside]*

> Poor Masetto is losing his temper,
> This whole thing has got quite out of hand.

DON GIOVANNI and LEPORELLO

> Look, Masetto is losing his temper
> It is more than his patience can stand.

MASETTO

> Don't you touch her, don't you touch her,
> This is more than my patience can stand.

> *[Enter Donna Anna, Donna Elvira and Don Ottavio, masked.]*

LEPORELLO

> Good evening, step this way, please,
> You charming masqueraders!

DON GIOVANNI

> Here everyone is welcome!
> Freedom for all, say I![24]

DONNA ANNA, DONNA ELVIRA and DON OTTAVIO

> We thank you for your greeting,
> And raise our glasses high.

ALL

> Freedom, freedom for all, say I!

DON GIOVANNI
Ricominciate il suono!

[a Leporello] Tu accoppia i ballerini.

LEPORELLO
Da bravi, via ballate!

DONNA ELVIRA *[a Donna Anna]*
Quella è la contadina.

DONNA ANNA *[a Don Ottavio]*
Io moro!

DON OTTAVIO *[a Donna Anna]*
Simulate!

DON GIOVANNI e LEPORELLO
Va bene in verità!

MASETTO *[ironicamente]*
Va bene, va bene, va bene in verità!

DON GIOVANNI *[a Leporello]*
A bada tien Masetto.

LEPORELLO *[a Masetto]*
Non balli, poveretto!
Vien qua, Masetto caro,
Facciam quel ch'altri fa.

DON GIOVANNI *[a Zerlina]*
Il tuo compagno io sono,
Zerlina, vien pur qua.

[Si mette a ballare una controdanza con Zerlina.]

MASETTO
No, no, ballar non voglio.

LEPORELLO
Eh, balla, amico mio!

MASETTO
No!

LEPORELLO
Sì, caro Masetto, balla!

DON GIOVANNI

Now we must have more music.

[to Leporello] Make sure they all have partners.

LEPORELLO

Come on, let's see you dancing.

DONNA ELVIRA *[to Donna Anna]*
Look there: it is Zerlina.

DONNA ANNA *[to Don Ottavio]*
Poor creature!

DON OTTAVIO *[to Donna Anna]*
Hush, he'll hear you.

DON GIOVANNI and LEPORELLO
It's going very well.

MASETTO *[ironically]*
Oh yes, sir, oh yes, sir, it's going very well.

DON GIOVANNI *[to Leporello]*
Get rid of that Masetto.

LEPORELLO *[to Masetto]*
Not dancing, poor Masetto?
If you can't find a partner, I'll do:
You'll have to dance with me.

DON GIOVANNI *[to Zerlina]*
Not dancing my Zerlina?
Zerlina, Zerlina, dance with me!

[They dance.]

MASETTO

You'll never catch me dancing.

LEPORELLO

Come on, now let's be friendly.

MASETTO

No!

LEPORELLO

Yes! Come on, Masetto, dance now!

MASETTO
No, no, non voglio!

DONNA ANNA
Resister non poss'io!

DONNA ELVIRA e DON OTTAVIO
Fingete per pietà!

LEPORELLO *[a Masetto]*
Balla!

MASETTO
No, no, non voglio!

LEPORELLO
Eh, balla, amico mio!
Facciam quel ch'altri fa.

[Vuol ballare con Masetto.]

DON GIOVANNI *[ballando conduce via Zerlina quasi per forza]*
Vieni con me, mia vita! Vieni, vieni!

MASETTO *[entra sciogliendosi da Leporello]*
Lasciami! Ah no! Zerlina!

ZERLINA
O numi! son tradita!

LEPORELLO
Qui nasce una ruina!

[Parte.]

DONNA ANNA, DONNA ELVIRA e DON OTTAVIO
L'iniquo da se stesso
Nel laccio se ne va!

ZERLINA *[di dentro]*
Gente, aiuto, aiuto! gente!

DONNA ANNA, DONNA ELVIRA e DON OTTAVIO
Soccorriamo l'innocente!

MASETTO *[di dentro]*
Ah, Zerlina!

ZERLINA *[Si sente il grido dalla parte opposta]*
Scellerato!

MASETTO
No, no, not likely.

DONNA ANNA
Oh no, I cannot bear it!

DONNA ELVIRA and DON OTTAVIO
You must, you must keep calm.

LEPORELLO *[to Masetto]*
Dance now!

MASETTO
No, no, not likely!

LEPORELLO
If you can't find a partner,
You'll have to dance with me.

[Leporello dances with Masetto.]

DON GIOVANNI *[dancing with Zerlina, forces her off]*
Let's slip away, my angel. Follow me now.

MASETTO *[escaping Leporello, follows them]*
Let me go. Oh no. Zerlina!

ZERLINA
Oh help me! He will ruin me!

LEPORELLO
This looks like a disaster!

[Hurries after them]

DONNA ANNA, DONNA ELVIRA and DON OTTAVIO
See how the villain tightens
The noose around his neck.

ZERLINA *[from inside]*
Help! Oh help, oh help, oh save me!

DONNA ANNA, DONNA ELVIRA and DON OTTAVIO
We must help her, we must save her!

MASETTO *[from within]*
My Zerlina!

ZERLINA *[from the other direction]*
Someone save me!

DONNA ANNA, DONNA ELVIRA e DON OTTAVIO
Ora grida da quel lato!

ZERLINA
Scellerato!

DONNA ANNA, DONNA ELVIRA e DON OTTAVIO
Ah gittiamo giù la porta!

ZERLINA
Soccorretemi! Ah, soccorretemi, o son morta!

DONNA ANNA, DONNA ELVIRA, DON OTTAVIO e MASETTO
Siam qui noi per tua difesa!

[Gettano giù la porta]

DON GIOVANNI *[esce con la spada in mano. Conduce seco per un braccio Leporello, e finge di voler ferirlo.]*

Ecco il birbo che t'ha offesa!
Ma da me la pena avrà! Mori, iniquo!

LEPORELLO
Ah, cosa fate?

DON GIOVANNI
Mori, dico!

LEPORELLO
Ah, cosa fate?

DON GIOVANNI
Mori, dico!

LEPORELLO
Ah, cosa fate?

DON OTTAVIO *[cavando una pistola]*
Noi sperate!

DONNA ANNA, DONNA ELVIRA e DON OTTAVIO
[si cavano la maschera]
L'empio crede con tal frode
Di nasconder l'empietà!

DON GIOVANNI
Donna Elvira!

DONNA ANNA, DONNA ELVIRA and DON OTTAVIO
  We must save her from his clutches!

ZERLINA
  Someone save me!

DONNA ANNA, DONNA ELVIRA and DON OTTAVIO
  We must go and break the door down!

ZERLINA
  Someone rescue me! Ah, set me free or I am ruined!

DONNA ANNA, DONNA ELVIRA, DON OTTAVIO and MASETTO
  We are coming to your rescue!

  [They succeed in breaking down the door, to expose . . .]

DON GIOVANNI *[with his sword in his hand. Leads Leporello out by the arm, and pretends to want to kill him.]*

  Here's the culprit. Here's your villain.
  But leave me to deal with him. You shall die, man!

LEPORELLO
  What are you doing?

DON GIOVANNI
  Death's your sentence!

LEPORELLO
  Have you gone crazy?

DON GIOVANNI
  Death's your sentence!

LEPORELLO
  But I've done nothing!

DON OTTAVIO *[drawing his pistol]*
  He is bluffing!

DONNA ELVIRA, DONNA ANNA and DON OTTAVIO *[unmasking]*
  Shame upon you for this outrage!
  We are here to make you pay.

DON GIOVANNI
  Donna Elvira?

DONNA ELVIRA

Si, malvaggio!

DON GIOVANNI

Don Ottavio!

DON OTTAVIO

Si, signore!

DON GIOVANNI

Ah credete . . .

DONNA ANNA, DONNA ELVIRA, ZERLINA, DON OTTAVIO
e MASETTO

Traditore! Tutto già si sà! Tutto!

Trema, trema, o scellerato!
Saprà tosto il mondo intero
Il misfatto orrendo e nero,
La tua fiera crudeltà!
Odi il tuon della vendetta,
Che ti fischia intorno intorno;
Sul tuo capo in questo giorno
Il suo fulmine cadrà.

LEPORELLO

È confusa la sua testa,
Non so più quel ch'ei si faccia:
E un orribile tempesta
Minacciando, o Dio, lo va.
Ma non manca in lui coraggio,
Non si perde o si confonde.
Se cadesse ancora il mondo,
Nulla mai temer lo fa.

DON GIOVANNI

È confusa la mia testa,
Non so più quel ch'io mi faccia;
E un orribile tempesta
Minacciando, o Dio, mi va.
Ma non manca in me coraggio,
Non mi perdo o mi confondo.
Se cadesse ancora il mondo,
Nulla mai temer mi fa.

102

DONNA ELVIRA

Yes, you monster!

DON GIOVANNI

Don Ottavio?

DON OTTAVIO

Yes indeed, sir!

DON GIOVANNI

Please believe me . . .

DONNA ANNA, DONNA ELVIRA, ZERLINA, DON OTTAVIO
and MASETTO

Foul seducer! Retribution is at hand. Vengeance![25]

Tremble, tremble, foul seducer!
We'll expose your guilty secrets.
And your dark satanic conduct
Will be known to one and all!
Hear the thunderbolt of vengeance,
Hear it crashing all around you;
On your head, now we have found you,
Mighty thunderbolts will fall.

LEPORELLO

He is dizzy with confusion.
There's no telling what may happen.
Round his head a storm is gath'ring
And a thunderbolt may fall.
But his courage will not fail him,
Nor will doubts and fears assail him,
Though the world itself should end now,
For he knows no fear at all.

DON GIOVANNI

I am dizzy with confusion.
There's no telling what may happen.
Round my head a storm is gath'ring
And a thunderbolt may fall.
But my courage will not fail me,
Nor will doubts and fears assail me,
Though the world itself should end now,
For I know no fear at all.

103

ATTO SECONDO

ACT TWO

SCENA I

[Strada]

N. 14 Duetto

DON GIOVANNI
Eh via, buffone, non mi seccar!

LEPORELLO
No, no, padrone, non vo' restar!

DON GIOVANNI
Sentimi, amico . . .

LEPORELLO
Vo' andar, vi dico!

DON GIOVANNI
Ma che ti ho fatto
Che vuoi lasciarmi?

LEPORELLO
O niente affatto,
Quasi ammazzarmi.

DON GIOVANNI
Va' che sei matto,
Fu per burlar.

LEPORELLO
Ed io non burlo,
Ma voglio andar.

[Va per partire.]

Recitativo

DON GIOVANNI
Leporello!

LEPORELLO
Signore?

DON GIOVANNI *[gli da del danaro]*
Vien qui, facciamo pace, prendi!

SCENE 1

[A street]

No. 14 Duet

DON GIOVANNI
  Have you gone crazy? What did you say?

LEPORELLO
  I am determined. I will not stay!

DON GIOVANNI
  Surely you're teasing!

LEPORELLO
  No, I am leaving!

DON GIOVANNI
  What have I done, then?
  Why be so angry?

LEPORELLO
  Oh nothing much, sir.
  Just tried to hang me!

DON GIOVANNI
  But I was joking.
  Was it not so?

LEPORELLO
  And I am serious.
  I want to go.

  [Makes to leave]

Recitative

DON GIOVANNI
  Leporello?

LEPORELLO
  Signore?

DON GIOVANNI [offering him money]
  Come here! Let's make it up. Take this!

LEPORELLO

Cosa?

DON GIOVANNI

Quattro doppie.

LEPORELLO

Oh, sentite: per questa volta la cerimonia accetto. Ma non vi ci avvezzate: non credete di sedurre i miei pari, come le donne, a forza di danari.

DON GIOVANNI

Non parliam più di ciò. Ti basta l'animo di far quel ch'io ti dico?

LEPORELLO

Purchè lasciam le donne.

DON GIOVANNI

Lasciar le donne! Pazzo! Lasciar le donne? Sai ch'elle per me son necessarie più del pan che mangio, più dell'aria che spiro!

LEPORELLO

E avete core d'ingannarle poi tutte?

DON GIOVANNI

È tutto amore: chi a una sola è fedele verso l'altre è crudele. Io, che in me sento sì esteso sentimento, vo' bene a tutte quante. Le donne, poi che calcolar non sanno, il mio buon natural chiamano inganno.

LEPORELLO

Non ho veduto mai naturale più vasto e più benigno. Orsù, cosa vorreste?

DON GIOVANNI

Odi: vedesti tu la cameriera di Donn' Elvira?

LEPORELLO

Io no.

DON GIOVANNI

Non hai veduto qualche cosa di bello caro il mio Leporello!

LEPORELLO

What's this?

DON GIOVANNI

Four gold sovereigns.

LEPORELLO

Oh, all right then. Just this once I'll forgive your wicked ways. But this must be the last time. I don't want you thinking you can charm me as you charm your women – not even with your money.

DON GIOVANNI

That's enough of that. So are you man enough to follow some instructions?

LEPORELLO

If you will give up women.

DON GIOVANNI

I give up women? Madman! I give up women? You know that I need them just as much as I need food and drink, or the air that I breathe!

LEPORELLO

And are you happy to leave them all broken-hearted?

DON GIOVANNI

It is my duty! To be faithful to one girl is unfair to the others. I have a heart so full of love and passion that I must subdivide it. But women's minds are not as sharp as men's are – if I share out my largesse, they call me faithless.

LEPORELLO

You're noted for your largesse, but I've never seen it shared out in such abundance. Now what was it you wanted?

DON GIOVANNI

Listen! You must have noticed the pretty handmaid of Donna Elvira?

LEPORELLO

Not me.

DON GIOVANNI

How could you miss her? She is really quite something. You must be going blind.[26] The time has come for me to try

109

Ora io con lei vo' tentar la mia sorte; ed ho pensato, giacchè siam verso sera, per aguzzarle meglio l'appetito di presentarmi a lei col tuo vestito.

LEPORELLO
E perchè non potreste presentarvi col vostro?

DON GIOVANNI
Han poco credito con gente di tal rango gli abiti signorili. Sbrigati, via!

LEPORELLO
Signor . . . per più ragioni . . .

DON GIOVANNI
Finiscila! Non soffro opposizioni!

[Leporello si mette l'abito di Don Giovanni.]

SCENA II

[si fa notte a poco a poco]

N. 15 Terzetto

DONNA ELVIRA *[alla finestra]*
   Ah taci, ingiusto core!
   Non palpitarmi in seno!
   È un empio, è un traditore,
   È colpa aver pietà.

LEPORELLO
   Zitto! di Donna Elvira,
   Signor, la voce io sento!

DON GIOVANNI
   Cogliere io vo' il momento,
   Tu fermati un po' là!

[Si mette dietro Leporello a parla a Donna Elvira.]

   Elvira, idolo mio!

DONNA ELVIRA
   Non è costui l'ingrato?

my luck, so I was thinking: the night is growing darker, and she might find me rather more attractive if I made love to her disguised as you.

LEPORELLO

And why can't you seduce her disguised as yourself?

DON GIOVANNI

Because these country girls associate a gentleman's hat and cloak with trouble. Take them off, quickly!

LEPORELLO

But, Signor, may I make so bold . . .

DON GIOVANNI

No, you may not! Just do as you are told!

[They exchange hats and cloaks.]

SCENE 2

[Night]

No. 15 Trio

DONNA ELVIRA *[at her window]*
    Ah, why this raging fever?[27]
    My heart beats all too wildly.
    He's heartless, he's a deceiver,
    I must not live in hope.

LEPORELLO
    Hush, master, did you hear that?
    It sounded like Donn' Elvira!

DON GIOVANNI
    Stand still, you fool. I hear her.
    I'll tempt her to elope.

    [Hides behind Leporello.]

    Elvira, I adore you!

DONNA ELVIRA
    Can that be the deceiver?

DON GIOVANNI

Sì, vita mia, son io,
E chiedo carità.

DONNA ELVIRA *[a parte]*

Numi, che strano affetto
Mi si risveglia in petto!

LEPORELLO

State a veder la pazza,
Che ancor gli crederà!

DON GIOVANNI

Discendi, o gioia bella,
Vedrai che tu sei quella
Che adora l'alma mia,
Pentito io sono già.

DONNA ELVIRA

No, non ti credo, o barbaro!

DON GIOVANNI

Ah credimi, o m'uccido!
Idolo mio, vien qua!

LEPORELLO *[piano, a Don Giovanni]*

Se seguitate, io rido!

DONNA ELVIRA

Dei, che cimento è questo!
Non so s'io vado o resto!
Ah proteggete voi
La mia credulità.

[Parte dalla finestra.]

DON GIOVANNI

Spero che cada presto!
Che bel colpetto è questo!
Più fertile talento
Del mio no non si dà!

LEPORELLO

Già quel mendace labbro
Torna a sedur costei,

DON GIOVANNI

Yes, here he's kneeling before you,
And pardon he implores.

DONNA ELVIRA *[aside]*

What is this strange emotion
Rekindling my devotion?

LEPORELLO

Watch how he still beguiles her;
She'll fall into his claws.

DON GIOVANNI

Come down, my only treasure!
Ahead lie hours of pleasure
As you and I rejoice.
Believe my repentant voice.

DONNA ELVIRA

No, you deceive me yet again!

DON GIOVANNI

Have faith in me or I'll kill myself!
Come to me, love, come down.

LEPORELLO *[quietly, to Don Giovanni]*

I'm breaking up with laughter.

DONNA ELVIRA

Ah, what a cruel dilemma!
Can I resist temptation?
Ah, heaven protect me
From my deluded heart.

[She leaves the window.]

DON GIOVANNI

How quickly she is falling.
She finds me so enthralling.
There's no one with my talent
For melting women's hearts.

LEPORELLO

With lies that are appalling
Her senses he's enthralling.

Deh proteggete, o dei!
La sua credulità!

Recitativo

DON GIOVANNI
Amico, che ti par?

LEPORELLO
Mi par che abbiate un'anima di bronzo.

DON GIOVANNI
Va là, che sei il gran gonzo! Ascolta bene: quando costei qui viene, tu corri ad abbracciarla, falle quattro carezze, fingi la voce mia: poi con bell'arte cerca teco condurla in altra parte.

LEPORELLO
Ma, signore . . .

DON GIOVANNI [mette presso il naso una pistola a Leporello]
Non piu repliche!

LEPORELLO
Ma se poi mi conosce?

DON GIOVANNI
Non ti conoscerà, se tu non vuoi, zitto, ell'apre, ehi, giudizio!

[Va in disparte. Entra Donna Elvira.]

SCENA III

DONNA ELVIRA
Eccomi a voi.

DON GIOVANNI [a parte]
Veggiamo che farà.

LEPORELLO [a parte]
Che imbroglio!

Ah, heaven protect her
From her deluded heart.

Recitative

DON GIOVANNI
So what d'you think of that?

LEPORELLO
I think it's monstrous. You have a heart of stone.[28]

DON GIOVANNI
You fool, don't waste your chances! Now listen closely:
when she comes out to find me, run over and embrace her,
smother her with your kisses, and imitate my voice. Then
think of some device to lead her away, so I'm alone here.

LEPORELLO
But, signore . . .

DON GIOVANNI *[puts his pistol to Leporello's temple]*
You protest too much!

LEPORELLO
What if she sees through me?

DON GIOVANNI
She won't if you hide your face;[29] it's up to you. Quiet,
she's coming. Eh, be careful!

[Don Giovanni hides. Enter Donna Elvira.]

SCENE 3

DONNA ELVIRA
Together at last!

DON GIOVANNI *[aside]*
This should be fun to watch![30]

LEPORELLO *[aside]*
He's dropped me in it this time!

DONNA ANNA

Dunque creder potrò che i pianti miei abbian vinto quel cor? Dunque pentito, l'amato Don Giovanni, al suo dovere e all'amor mio ritorna?

LEPORELLO [imitando la voce di Don Giovanni]

Sì, carina!

DONNA ELVIRA

Crudele, se sapeste quante lagrime e quanti sospir voi mi costate!

LEPORELLO

Io mia vita?

DONNA ELVIRA

Voi.

LEPORELLO

Poverina! Quanto mi dispiace!

DONNA ELVIRA

Mi fuggirete più?

LEPORELLO

No, muso bello.

DONNA ELVIRA

Sarete sempre mio?

LEPORELLO

Sempre!

DONNA ELVIRA

Carissimo!

LEPORELLO

Carissima!
[a parte] La burla mi dà gusto.

DONNA ELVIRA

Mio tesoro!

LEPORELLO

Mia Venere!

DONNA ELVIRA

Son per voi tutta foco.

DONNA ELVIRA

Can I dare to believe that all my suffering has at last touched your heart? And can it be that a repentant Don Giovanni will do his duty and marry his Elvira?

LEPORELLO *[imitating the voice of Don Giovanni]*

Yes, my darling!

DONNA ELVIRA

You cruel one! If you knew how much I've missed you, how many tearful sighs you've cost me!

LEPORELLO

I, my beloved?

DONNA ELVIRA

Yes, you.

LEPORELLO

My poor darling! This is too distressing!

DONNA ELVIRA

You'll never leave again?

LEPORELLO

No, my Venus!³¹

DONNA ELVIRA

You promise to be faithful?

LEPORELLO

Always!

DONNA ELVIRA

Oh, ecstasy!

LEPORELLO

Oh, ecstasy!
[aside] I'm beginning to enjoy this!

DONNA ELVIRA

My only treasure!

LEPORELLO

My Juliet!³²

DONNA ELVIRA

I'm aflame with desire.

LEPORELLO
Io tutto cenere.

DON GIOVANNI *[a parte]*
Il birbo si riscalda.

DONNA ELVIRA
E non m'ingannerete?

LEPORELLO
No, sicuro.

DONNA ELVIRA
Giuratemi.

LEPORELLO
Lo giuro a questa mano, che bacio con trasporto, a quei bei lumi.

DON GIOVANNI *[fingendo di uccidere qualcheduno]*
Ih! Eh! Ih! Ah! Sei morto!

DONNA ELVIRA e LEPORELLO
Oh numi!

[Fuggono.]

DON GIOVANNI *[ridendo]*
Ih! Eh! Ih! Eh! Ih! Ah!
Purchè la sorte mi secondi; veggiamo!
Le finestre son queste; ora cantiamo.

N. 16 Canzonetta

DON GIOVANNI
Deh vieni alla finestra, o mio tesoro,
Deh vieni a consolar il pianto mio.
Se neghi a me di dar qualche ristoro,
Davanti agli occhi tuoi morir vogl'io!

Tu ch'hai la bocca dolce più che il miele,
Tu che il zucchero porti in mezzo il core!
Non esser, gioia mia, con me crudele!
Lasciati almen veder, mio bell'amore!

LEPORELLO

  I'm burnt to cinders.

DON GIOVANNI *[aside]*

  He's warming to his task now!

DONNA ELVIRA

  You promise not to cheat me?

LEPORELLO

  Yes, I promise.

DONNA ELVIRA

  You'll swear to that?

LEPORELLO

  I swear it by your hand, and seal it with a kiss here . . . and
  with another . . .

DON GIOVANNI *[pretending to be ambushed]*

  Ih! Eh! Ah! Ih! Take that, you . . . !

DONNA ELVIRA and LEPORELLO

  Lord save us!

  [Exeunt hurriedly.]

DON GIOVANNI *[laughing]*

  Ih! Eh! Ih! Ah! Ih!
  It seems my fortunes are improving! That's better . . .
  This must be the window. I'll sing a canzonetta!

No. 16 Canzonetta

DON GIOVANNI

  Throw open wide your window, for I adore you;
  Come down here to console my lonely sighing.
  In hope of some relief I stand before you,
  Or else before your eyes you'll see me dying.

  Your lips of honey promise tastes of pleasure;
  Juices sweeter than nectar flow from your heart above.
  Be cruel to me no more, my only treasure,
  Just for one moment let me glimpse the face I love.

Recitativo

V'è gente alla finestra: forse dessa! Zi, zi!

SCENA IV

[Masetto, armato d'archibuso e pistola, Contadine e detto]

MASETTO
Non ci stanchiamo; il cor mi dice che trovarlo dobbiam.

DON GIOVANNI *[a parte]*
Qualcuno parla!

MASETTO
Fermatevi; mi pare che alcuno qui si muova.

DON GIOVANNI *[a parte]*
Se non fallo, è Masetto!

MASETTO
Chi va là? Non risponde; animo, schioppo al muso! Chi va
là?

DON GIOVANNI *[a parte]*
Non è solo; ci vuol giudizio. *[Cerca d'imitare la voce di
Leporello]* Amici. *[a parte] Non mi voglio scoprir. [a Masetto]*
Sei tu Masetto?

MASETTO
Appunto quello: e tu?

DON GIOVANNI
Non mi conosci? Il servo son io di Don Giovanni.

MASETTO
Leporello, servo di quell' indegno cavaliere!

DON GIOVANNI
Certo; di quel briccone!

Recitative

There's someone at the window! Could it be her? Hello there!

SCENE 4

[Enter Masetto, armed with gun and pistol; accompanied by villagers, also armed.]

MASETTO

Don't let's give up. Something tells me he's not far away.

DON GIOVANNI *[aside]*

There's someone coming!

MASETTO

Stop, everyone! I think there's someone in the shadows!

DON GIOVANNI *[aside]*

It sounds like Masetto.

MASETTO

Who goes there? No one answers. Friends, weapons at the ready! Who goes there?

DON GIOVANNI *[aside]*

There are others. I must be careful . . . *[imitating the voice of Leporello]* A friend! *[aside]* They must not see it's me! *[to Masetto]* Is that Masetto?

MASETTO

Yes, I'm Masetto. And you?

DON GIOVANNI

Surely you know me? You've seen me enough with Don Giovanni.

MASETTO

Leporello! Servant of that loathsome cavalier!

DON GIOVANNI

That's right, he is quite shameless.

MASETTO

Di quell' uom senza onore: ah, dimmi un poco, dove possiam trovarlo; lo cerco con costor per trucidarlo!

DON GIOVANNI

[a parte] Bagatelle! *[a Masetto]* Bravissimo, Masetto! Anch'io con voi m'unisco per fargliela a quel birbo di padrone; or senti un po' qual è la mia intenzione.

N. 17 Aria

Metà di voi qua vadano,
E gli altri vadan là!
I pian pianin lo cerchino,
Lontan non sia di quà!
Se un uom e una ragazza
Passeggian per la piazza,
Se sotto a una finestra
Fare all'amor sentite,
Ferite pur, ferite.
Il mio padron sarà
In testa egli ha un cappello.
Con candidi pennacchi,
Addosso un gran mantello,
E spada al fianco egli ha,
Andate, fate presto,
To sol verrai con me.
Noi far dobbiamo il resto,
E gia vedrai cos'è.

[Partono i contadini da opposte vie.]

SCENA V

Recitativo

DON GIOVANNI

Zitto, lascia ch'io senta! Ottimamente: dunque dobbiam ucciderlo?

MASETTO

Yes, that lecherous devil . . . Ah, tell me quickly where might I find him lurking? My friends and I intend to blow his brains out.

DON GIOVANNI

[aside] How delightful! *[to Masetto]* Well, good for you, Masetto! I'd like to come and help you. It's time I got my own back on my master. I have an idea which might help you catch him faster.

No. 17 Aria

Let half of you look over there,
The rest the other way,
And softly, softly seek him out:
He can't be far away.
If some of you discover
A woman with her lover
Or see beneath a window
A suitor taking cover,[33]
Attack him, then, attack him,
It's sure to be my lord.
You'll know him by his swagger,
His cloak and hat with feathers.
He sometimes wears a dagger,
But always bears a sword.
You quickly go and find him,
And you remain with me.
We'll finish off this business,
You leave the rest to me.

[Don Giovanni and Masetto are left alone.]

SCENE 5

Recitative

DON GIOVANNI

Ssh! Be quiet a moment! Couldn't be better! So you intend to kill him?

MASETTO

Sicuro!

DON GIOVANNI

E non ti basteria rompergli l'ossa, fracassargli le spalle?

MASETTO

No, no, voglio ammazzarlo, vo' farlo in cento brani.

DON GIOVANNI

Hai buon'arme?

MASETTO

Cospetto! Ho pria questo moschetto, e poi questa pistola.
[Da moschetto e pistola a Don Giovanni.]

DON GIOVANNI

E poi?

MASETTO

Non basta?

DON GIOVANNI

Oh, basta certo; or prendi, questa per la pistola, questa per il moschetto!

[Batte Masetto col rovescio della spada.]

MASETTO

Ahi! ahi! soccorso! ahi! ahi!

DON GIOVANNI

Taci, o sei morto! Questi per ammazzarlo, questi per farlo in brani! Villano, mascalzon! Ceffo da cani!

SCENA VI

MASETTO

Ahi! ahi! la testa mia! Ahi, le spalle! E il petto!

MASETTO

Indeed I do!

DON GIOVANNI

Wouldn't it be enough to break a few bones, give him something to remember?[34]

MASETTO

No, no; I want to murder him, and then cut him up in pieces . . .

DON GIOVANNI

Are you well armed?

MASETTO

I'll show you! I've brought my musket with me, and also this big pistol. *[Hands them to Don Giovanni.]*

DON GIOVANNI

Is that all?

MASETTO

Won't these do?

DON GIOVANNI

Yes, they'll do nicely. Take that then! This one is for the pistol; this one is for the musket.

[Beats him.]

MASETTO

Ahi! Ahi! My head, my head!

DON GIOVANNI

Silence, or I'll kill you. This one's for plotting murder, this one for trespassing in his grounds! You impudent wretch, I'll feed you to his hounds!

SCENE 6

MASETTO

Ahi, Ahi! What has he done to me? Oh my God! My shoulders, my ribs!

ZERLINA

Di sentire mi parve la voce di Masetto!

MASETTO

O Dio, Zerlina, Zerlina mia, soccorso!

ZERLINA

Cosa è stato?

MASETTO

L'iniquo, il scellerato mi ruppe l'ossa e i nervi.

ZERLINA

Oh poveretta me! Chi?

MASETTO

Leporello! o qualche diavol che somiglia a lui!

ZERLINA

Crudel, non tel diss'io che con questa tua pazza gelosia ti ridurresti a qualche brutto passo? Dove ti duole?

MASETTO

Qui.

ZERLINA

E poi?

MASETTO

Qui, e ancora qui!

ZERLINA

E poi non ti duol altro?

MASETTO

Duolmi un poco questo piè, questo braccio, e questa mano.

ZERLINA

Via, via, non è gran mal, se il resto è sano. Vientene meco a casa; purchè tu mi prometta d'essere men geloso, io, io ti guarirò, caro il mio sposo.

ZERLINA

Do I hear someone groaning? I hope it's not Masetto!

MASETTO

Oh God, Zerlina! Zerlina darling, oh help me!

ZERLINA

What has happened?

MASETTO

The bastard, he beat me up, and broke every bone in my body.

ZERLINA

Who'd do a thing like that? Who?

MASETTO

Leporello! Or some evil creature dressed up in his clothes.

ZERLINA

You fool! Didn't I tell you that this jealousy of yours was total madness, and in the end it would get you into trouble? Where did he hit you?

MASETTO

Here.

ZERLINA

And where else?

MASETTO

Here . . . and here too . . . here.

ZERLINA

And nothing else is damaged?

MASETTO

Yes, he's hurt me on the leg, on my arm here, and on my hand.

ZERLINA

Come on, it's not so bad if the rest still works. Come, let me take you home now. If you can promise me not to be so suspicious, I'll promise you a cure you'll find delicious.

N. 18 Aria

ZERLINA

Vedrai carino, se sei buonino,
Che bel rimedio ti voglio dar!
È naturale, non dà disgusto.
E lo speziale non lo sa far.
È un certo balsamo ch'io porto addosso,
Dare te'l posso, Se'l vuoi provar.
Saper vorresti dove mi sta?
Sentilo battere, toccami qua!

[Partono.]

SCENA VII

[Atrio terreno oscuro in casa di Donna Anna]

Recitativo

LEPORELLO

Di molte faci il lume s'avvicina, o mio ben; stiamci qui,
ascosi, finchè da noi si scosta.

DONNA ELVIRA

Ma che temi, adorato mio sposo?

LEPORELLO

Nulla, nulla – certi riguardi, io vo' veder se il lume è già
lontano. *[A parte]* Ah, come da costei liberarmi? *[A Donna
Elvira]* Rimanti, anima bella!

DONNA ELVIRA

Ah! Non lasciarmi!

N. 19 Sextet

DONNA ELVIRA

Sola, sola in buio loco
Palpitar il cor mi sento,
E m'assale un tal spavento,
Che mi sembra di morir.

No. 18 Aria

ZERLINA

You'll see, my darling, if you will trust me,
There is a remedy I can supply.
It is quite painless. You'll find it soothing.
It's an elixir money can't buy.
There is a treatment known to me only,
Treatment I'm sure that you'll want to try.
Where do I hide it? Very near by.
Feel my heart beating here, soon you'll know why.

[Exit Zerlina and Masetto.]

SCENE 7

[a dark hall in Donna Anna's house]

Recitative

LEPORELLO *[still pretending to be Don Giovanni]*

I'm sure I see some lanterns approaching us, my love. Keep
in the shadows; maybe they'll go away soon.

DONNA ELVIRA

Why be frightened? Does it matter, my darling?

LEPORELLO

Not exactly . . . just being careful. I'll go and see if they
have disappeared yet. *[aside]* Ah, how can I get rid of this
harpy? *[to Donna Elvira]* Stay here, oh most beloved.

DONNA ELVIRA

Ah, do not leave me!

No. 19 Sextet

DONNA ELVIRA

All alone, alone in darkness,
My poor senses all are reeling.
There assails me so dread a feeling
I'm afraid that I might die.

LEPORELLO
Più che cerco, men ritrovo
Questa porta sciagurata;
Piano, piano, l'ho trovata!
Ecco il tempo di fuggir!

[Donna Anna e Don Ottavio entrano vestiti a lutto]

DON OTTAVIO
Tergi il ciglio, o vita mia,
E da' calma al tuo dolore!
L'ombra omai del genitore
Pena avrà de'tuoi martir.

DONNA ANNA
Lascia almen alla mia pena
Questo picciolo ristoro;
Sola morte, o mio tesoro,
Il mio pianto può finir.

DONNA ELVIRA *[senza esser vista]*
Ah dov'è lo sposo mio?

LEPORELLO *[ancha esser vista]*
Se mi trova, son perduto!

DONNA ELVIRA e LEPORELLO
Una porta là vegg'io,
Cheto cheto vo' partir!

[Nel partir s'incontra con Zerlina e Masetto.]

SCENA VIII

ZERLINA e MASETTO
Ferma, briccone, dove ten vai?

DONNA ANNA e DON OTTAVIO
Ecco il fellone, com'era qua?

DONNA ANNA, ZERLINA, DON OTTAVIO e MASETTO
Ah, mora il perfido! Che m'ha tradito!

LEPORELLO

Where's that doorway? I can't find it!
It was here, I must be searching all around it.
Wait a moment: I have found it.
Now is the time for me to fly.

[Enter Don Ottavio and Donna Anna, dressed in mourning.]

DON OTTAVIO

My beloved, cease your weeping,
Put an end to such deep mourning.
I know your father would not wish it.
Dry your tears, you weep in vain.

DONNA ANNA

Leave me, leave me to my sorrow
And my bitter desolation.
Only dying, my beloved
Could put an end to all my pain.

DONNA ELVIRA [unseen]

Ah, my love, where have you gone to?

LEPORELLO [also unseen]

If they find me, I am ruined!

DONNA ELVIRA and LEPORELLO

Ah, I think I see a doorway.
Here's my chance to slip away.

[Leporello, while trying to escape, bumps into Zerlina and
Masetto.]

SCENE 8

ZERLINA and MASETTO

Stay there, you ruffian! You can't escape us!

DONNA ANNA and DON OTTAVIO

That's Don Giovanni! Why is he here?

DONNA ANNA, ZERLINA, DON OTTAVIO and MASETTO

Death to the murderer, to the deceiver!

DONNA ELVIRA

   È mio marito! Pietà!

DONNA ANNA, ZERLINA, DON OTTAVIO e MASETTO

   È Donna Elvira?
   Quella ch'io vedo?
   Appena il credo!

DONNA ELVIRA

   Pietà, pietà!

TUTTI

   No! Morrà!

   [Don Ottavio in atto di ucciderlo; Leporello si scopre e si mette in ginocchio]

LEPORELLO

   Perdon, perdono, signori miei!
   Quello io non sono, sbaglia costei!
   Viver lasciatemi per carità!

TUTTI

   Dei! Leporello! Che inganno è questo!
   Stupido resto! Che mai sarà?

LEPORELLO

   Mille torbidi pensieri
   Mi s'aggiran per la testa;
   Se mi salvo in tal tempesta,
   È un prodigio in verità.

TUTTI

   Mille torbidi pensieri
   Mi s'aggiran per la testa;
   Che giornata, o stelle, è questa!
   Che impensata novità!

   [Parte Donna Anna.]

DONNA ELVIRA

He is my husband.[35] Be kind, and grant reprieve!

DONNA ANNA, ZERLINA, DON OTTAVIO and MASETTO

It's Donn' Elvira!
Has love deceived her?
I cannot believe her.

DONNA ELVIRA

Reprieve, reprieve!

ALL

No! He dies!

[Don Ottavio makes to kill him; Leporello reveals himself and falls to his knees.]

LEPORELLO

Forgive, forgive me! I beg your mercy!
I'm not Giovanni. She has misled you.
Spare me my life, I pray, for pity's sake.

ALL

God! Leporello? He has deceived us.
I don't believe this. What can it mean?

LEPORELLO

Round my head a storm is raging,
Showering doubts and fears upon me.
If I cannot escape the gallows
I will be on my way to hell.

ALL

Round my head a storm is raging,
Showering doubts and fears upon me.
What confusion today has witnessed!
What will follow I can't tell.

[Exit Donna Anna.]

SCENA IX

Recitativo

ZERLINA

Dunque quello sei tu, che il mio Masetto poco fà crudelmente maltrattasti!

DONNA ELVIRA

Dunque tu m'ingannasti, o scellerato, spacciandoti con me da Don Giovanni.

DON OTTAVIO

Dunque tu in questi panni venisti qui per qualche tradimento!

DONNA ELVIRA

A me tocca punirlo.

ZERLINA

Anzi a me.

DON OTTAVIO

No, no, a me.

MASETTO

Accoppatelo meco tutti tre.

N. 20 Aria

LEPORELLO

Ah, pietà! signori miei!
Ah, pietà, pietà di me!
Do ragione a voi, e lei,
Ma il delitto mio non è.
Il padron con prepotenza,
L'innocenza mi rubò.

[a Donna Elvira]

Donna Elvira, compatite!
Già capite come andò.
Già capite, già capite,
Già capite come andò.

SCENE 9

Recitative

ZERLINA

It was you, then, who just gave my Masetto such a beating
that it very nearly killed him?

DONNA ELVIRA

It was you that just tricked me, you dissembler, by dressing
yourself up as Don Giovanni?

DON OTTAVIO

Pretended to be your master, so that you might get away
with yet more evil?

DONNA ELVIRA

Let me see that he's punished.

ZERLINA

No, let me.

DON OTTAVIO

No, no, let me.

MASETTO

Let us all see he never more goes free.

No. 20 Aria

LEPORELLO

Ah, you must be kind to me,
Ah, be kind, be kind to me.
You have reason to be so angry,
But the offender was not me.
Don Giovanni's such a tyrant
That I dared not disobey.

[to Donna Elvira]

Donn' Elvira, do forgive me, do forgive me.
What he's like I needn't say
For you know him, yes, you know him.
What he's like I needn't say.

[a Zerlina]

Di Masetto non so nulla,
Vel dirà questa fanciulla.
È un oretta circumcirca,
Che con lei girando vò.

[a Don Ottavio]

A voi, signore, non dico niente,
Certo timore, certo accidente,
Di fuori chiaro, di dentro scuro,
Non c'è riparo, la porta, il muro,
Lo . . . il . . . la . . .
Vò da quel lato, poi qui celato,
L'affar si sa . . . oh, si sa . . .
Ma s'io sapeva, fuggia per quà,
Fuggia per qua, fuggia per quà!

[S'avvicina con destrezza alla porta e fugge]

SCENA X

Recitativo

DONNA ELVIRA
Ferma, perfido, ferma!

MASETTO
Il birbo ha l'ali ai piedi!

ZERLINA
Con qual arte si sottrasse l'iniquo.

DON OTTAVIO
Amici miei, dopo eccessi sì enormi, dubitar non possiam che
Don Giovanni non sia l'empio uccisore del padre di Donna
Anna; in questa casa per poche ore fermatevi, un ricorso
vo'far a chi si deve, e in pochi istanti vendicarvi prometto.
Così vuole dover, pietade, affetto!

[to Zerlina]

Of Masetto I know nothing,
As this lady is my witness.
We've been walking, yes, and talking,
This past hour I've spent with her.

[to Don Ottavio]

To you my conduct I'm not excusing . . .
I was so frightened . . . it was confusing . . .
I saw some shadows . . . I was in darkness . . .
I was surrounded . . . the doorway . . . the darkness . . .
It . . . well . . . she . . .
I tried the door here, then tried one more here.
What can I say? What to say?
But I just might have escaped this way,
Perhaps this way, perhaps this way.

[Escapes]

SCENE 10

Recitative

DONNA ELVIRA

Stop that criminal, stop him!

MASETTO

He's vanished into thin air.

ZERLINA

He's so crafty that he's slipped through our fingers.

DON OTTAVIO

My friends, it's clear now, after all we have witnessed: there is no doubt at all that Don Giovanni was the cruel assassin of Donna Anna's father. I advise you all to stay together, for your own protection, while I go and report this dreadful story. And very soon we'll accomplish our mission. Love and duty demand that he go to perdition.

N. 21 Aria

Il mio tesoro intanto
Andate a consolar.
E del bel ciglio il pianto
Cercate di asciugar.

Ditele che i suoi torti
A vendicar io vado;
Che sol di stragi e morti
Nunzio vogl'io tornar.

[Partono Zerlina, Don Ottavio e Masetto.]

N. 21b Recitativo accompagnato ed Aria

DONNA ELVIRA

In quali eccessi, o Numi, in quai misfatti orribili, tremendi, è avvolto il sciagurato! Ah no, non puote tardar l'ira del cielo! . . . la giustizia tardar. Sentir già parmi la fatale saetta, che piomba sul capo! Aperto veggio il baratro mortal! Misera Elvira! Che contrasto d'affetti, in sen ti nasce! Perchè questi sospiri? E queste ambascie?

Mi tradì, quell'alma ingrata,
Infelice, o Dio, mi fa,
Ma tradita e abbandonata,
Provo ancor per lui pietà.

Quando sento il mio tormento,
Di vendetta il cor favella,
Ma se guardo il suo cimento,
Palpitando il cor mi va.

[Parte.]

No. 21 Aria

Comfort my treasure 'till I return,
Compassion would have it so.
Wipe from her eyes those teardrops,
Console her in her woe.

Tell her I do her bidding;
I shall avenge her father.
The murd'rer shall be punished;
Justice demands I go.

[Exeunt Zerlina, Don Ottavio, and Masetto.]

No. 21b Accompanied Recitative and Aria

DONNA ELVIRA

To what excesses, Oh heaven, to what disgraceful depths of immorality that sinner has descended. Ah no! No longer can he avoid retribution, and escape heaven's wrath. I see already the arrows of vengeance that will rain down upon him. Before him opens the gaping mouth of hell. Wretched Elvira, why in such sad confusion must you still languish? Ah, why this ceaseless sighing, and why such anguish?

Ev'ry word was vain and deceitful,
Each vow empty, each promise a lie.
He betrayed me, left me abandoned,
Yet my love will never die.

For my lonely desolation,
My whole heart cries out for vengeance.
Yet it races with trepidation,
And true love alone knows why.

[Exit.]

SCENA XI

*[Loco chiuso in forma di sepolcreto. Diverse statue
equestri: statua del Commendatore]*

Recitativo

DON GIOVANNI *[entra pel muretto ridendo]*
Ah, ah, ah, questa è buona, or lasciala cercar; che bella
notte! È più chiara del giorno, sembra fatta per gir a zonzo a
caccia di ragazze. È tardi? Oh, ancor non sono due della
notte; avrei voglia un po' di saper come è finito l'affar tra
Leporello e Donna Elvira: s'egli ha avuto giudizio!

LEPORELLO *[si affaccia al muretto]*
Alfin vuole ch'io faccia un precipizio.

DON GIOVANNI
È desso. Eh, Leporello!

LEPORELLO *[dal muro]*
Chi mi chiama?

DON GIOVANNI
Non conosci il padron?

LEPORELLO
Così nol conoscessi!

DON GIOVANNI
Come, birbo?

LEPORELLO
Ah, siete voi? Scusate.

DON GIOVANNI
Cosa è stato?

LEPORELLO
Per cagion vostra io fui quasi accoppato.

DON GIOVANNI
Ebben, non era questo un onore per te?

LEPORELLO
Signor, vel dono.

SCENE 11

[A walled cemetery. Among the monuments is a statue of the Commendatore.]

Recitative

DON GIOVANNI *[enters over the wall, laughing]*
Ah! Ah! Ah! This is perfect! She'll never find me here. How bright the moon is; it is clearer than daylight; just the night to be out here prowling around for pretty women. How late is it? Oh, still quite early, not even two yet. I'm dying to know what eventually happened between Leporello and Donna Elvira. All that billing and cooing!

LEPORELLO *[from outside]*
He's determined to be my undoing.

DON GIOVANNI
He's here. Oh, Leporello!

LEPORELLO *[from the wall]*
Who wants him?

DON GIOVANNI
Don't you recognise your master?

LEPORELLO
I really wish I didn't!

DON GIOVANNI
What's that, you rascal?

LEPORELLO
Ah, is that you? Excuse me!

DON GIOVANNI
What has happened?

LEPORELLO
Because of you I was almost a dead man.

DON GIOVANNI
Wasn't that an honour – to be taken for me?

LEPORELLO
Signor, some honour!

141

DON GIOVANNI

Via, via, vien qua; che belle cose ti deggio dir.

LEPORELLO

Ma cosa fate qui?

DON GIOVANNI

Vien dentro e lo saprai: diverse istorielle che accadute mi son dacche partisti, ti dirò un' altra volta: or la più bella ti vo' solo narrar.

[Leporello entra; si cangiano d'abito]

LEPORELLO

Donnesca al certo?

DON GIOVANNI

C'è dubbio? Una fanciulla, bella, giovin, galante, per la strada incontrai; le vado appresso, la prendo per la man, fuggir mi vuole; dico poche parole, ella mi piglia, sai per chi?

LEPORELLO

Non lo so.

DON GIOVANNI

Per Leporello.

LEPORELLO

Per me?

DON GIOVANNI

Per te.

LEPORELLO

Va bene.

DON GIOVANNI

Per la mano essa allora mi prende.

LEPORELLO

Ancora meglio.

DON GIOVANNI

Come, come listen to me. I have amazing things to tell you.

LEPORELLO

But what are you doing here?

DON GIOVANNI

Come here and you shall know. So many things have happened since we parted and went our separate ways. They can wait until later; meanwhile, there's one piece of news you have to hear.

[Leporello comes from the wall; they exchange clothes.]

LEPORELLO

Another woman!

DON GIOVANNI

You guessed it. This one is gorgeous: very young, very pretty, walking down the street beside me: so I go up to her, I take her by the hand; she tries to escape me. So I whisper in her ear, and she mistakes me for . . . guess who?[36]

LEPORELLO

I don't know.

DON GIOVANNI

For Leporello.

LEPORELLO

For me?

DON GIOVANNI

For you!

LEPORELLO

Terrific!

DON GIOVANNI

So now it's *she* who takes *me* by the hand . . .

LEPORELLO

Even better . . .

DON GIOVANNI

M'accarezza, mi abbraccia: 'Caro il mio Leporello! Leporello, mio caro!' Allor m'accorsi ch'era qualche tua bella.

LEPORELLO *[a parte]*

Oh maledetto!

DON GIOVANNI

Dell'inganno approfitto; non so come mi riconosce, grida; sento gente, a fuggire mi metto, e pronto pronto per quel muretto in questo loco io monto.

LEPORELLO

E mi dite la cosa con tale indifferenza?

DON GIOVANNI

Perchè no?

LEPORELLO

Ma se fosse costei stata mia moglie?

DON GIOVANNI *[ridendo forte]*

Ancora meglio!

COMMENDATORE

Di rider finirai pria dell'aurora!

DON GIOVANNI

Chi ha parlato?

LEPORELLO

Ah, qualche anima sarà dell'altro mondo, che vi conosce a fondo.

DON GIOVANNI

Taci, sciocco! Chi va là?

COMMENDATORE

Ribaldo, audace! Lascia a'morti la pace!

LEPORELLO

Ve l'ho detto!

DON GIOVANNI

She caresses me, embraces me, 'O darling Leporello, Leporello my darling . . .' And then I realise that she must be your mistress.

LEPORELLO *[aside]*

Hell and damnation!

DON GIOVANNI

I am making the most of it, but then somehow she recognises me; cries out; I hear voices; so I take to my heels, and quickly, quickly, jump over the wall and find myself in this place.

LEPORELLO

And you're telling me this without a single pang of conscience?

DON GIOVANNI

Yes, why not?

LEPORELLO

But supposing this girl had been my wife?

DON GIOVANNI

Even better! *[laughs cruelly]*

COMMENDATORE

Your laughter will be over by the morning!

DON GIOVANNI

Who said that?

LEPORELLO

Ah! It must have been some spirit sent from Hell who knows all about you.

DON GIOVANNI

Don't be foolish! Who goes there?

COMMENDATORE

Blasphemer, take warning! Let the dead rest in silence!

LEPORELLO

What did I tell you?

DON GIOVANNI

Sarà qualcun di fuori che si burla di noi! Ehi, del Commendatore non è questa la statua? Leggi un poco quella iscrizion.

LEPORELLO

Scusate, non ho imparato a leggere a'raggi della luna.

DON GIOVANNI

Leggi, dico!

LEPORELLO [legge]

'Dell'empio che mi trasse al passo estremo qui attendo la vendetta.' Udiste? Io tremo!

DON GIOVANNI

O vecchio buffonissimo! Digli che questa sera l'attendo a cenar meco!

LEPORELLO

Che pazzia! Ma vi par . . . oh Dei, mirate, che terribili occhiate egli ci dà! Par vivo! Par che senta, e che voglia parlar!

DON GIOVANNI

Orsù, va là! o qui t'ammazzo, e poi ti seppellisco!

LEPORELLO

Piano, piano signore, ora ubbidisco.

N. 22 Duetto

LEPORELLO

O statua gentilissima
Del gran Commendatore . . .

[a Don Giovanni]

Padron! Mi trema il core,
Non posso terminar!

DON GIOVANNI

Finiscila, o nel petto
Ti metto questo acciar!

DON GIOVANNI

It must be someone out there who is playing a joke on us!
Look, the Commendatore makes a very handsome statue!
Go on, read me the inscription.

LEPORELLO

Excuse me: I never learnt to read too well, especially by
moonlight.

DON GIOVANNI

Go on, read it!

LEPORELLO *[reading the inscription]*

'Upon the impious coward who caused my downfall I wait
here for my vengeance.' Did you hear that? I'm frightened!

DON GIOVANNI

I thought we'd seen the last of him! Tell him to come to
dinner with me this very evening.

LEPORELLO

Are you mad? But you can't . . . Oh God, I'm sure that he is
glaring at us with his stony eyes! You'd think that he was
listening, and waiting to reply . . .

DON GIOVANNI

Do as I say, or I will kill you and put you there beside him!

LEPORELLO

Take it easy, my lord, I will invite him!

No. 22 Duet

LEPORELLO

O most respected monument
To our Commendatore . . .

(to Don Giovanni)

Oh no! I feel so frightened
I cannot carry on.

DON GIOVANNI

Get on with it. You invite him
Or you'll be dead and gone.

LEPORELLO

Che impiccio, che capriccio!

DON GIOVANNI

Che gusto, che spassetto!

LEPORELLO

Io sentomi gelar!

DON GIOVANNI

Lo voglio far tremar!

LEPORELLO

O statua gentilissima,
Benchè di marmo siate . . .
Ah padron! Padron mio! Mirate!
Che seguita a guardar!

DON GIOVANNI

Mori, mori!

LEPORELLO

No, attendete!
Signor, il padron mio,
Badate ben, non io,
Vorria con voi cenar!

[La statua china la testa.]

Ah, che scena è questa!
O ciel! Chinò la testa!

DON GIOVANNI

Va là, che sei un buffone!

LEPORELLO

Guardate ancor, padrone!

DON GIOVANNI

E che deggio guardar?

DON GIOVANNI e LEPORELLO

Colla marmorea testa,
Ei fa così, così!

DON GIOVANNI *[alla statua]*

Parlate, se potete.
Verrete a cena?

LEPORELLO

How crazy, how capricious!

DON GIOVANNI

How funny, how delicious!

LEPORELLO

My blood is running cold!

DON GIOVANNI

He'll do as he is told!

LEPORELLO

O most respected monument,
Although you're made of marble . . .
No, I can't! I can't do it! The statue . . .
I saw him move his eyes!

DON GIOVANNI

Coward! Coward!

LEPORELLO

No, wait, I'll do it!
If you would care to dine, sir . . .
It's his idea, not mine, sir . . .
My lord suggests tonight.

[The statue nods its head.]

Ah, I can't believe it,
Oh God, his head is nodding.

DON GIOVANNI

He's frightened of a statue!

LEPORELLO

Those eyeballs stare right at you!

DON GIOVANNI

You fool, there's nothing there.

DON GIOVANNI and LEPORELLO

Even though made of marble,
He nods his head like this.

DON GIOVANNI *[to the statue]*

So answer, if you're able:
You'll come to dinner?

COMMENDATORE

Sì!

DON GIOVANNI

Bizzarra è in ver la scena,
Verrà il buon vecchio a cena.
A prepararla andiamo,
Partiamo via di qua!

LEPORELLO

Mover mi posso appena
Mi manca, o Dei, la lena!
Per carità, partiamo,
Andiamo via di qua!

[Partono.]

SCENA XII

[Camera tetra]

Recitativo

DON OTTAVIO

Calmatevi, idol mio! Di quel ribaldo vedrem puniti in breve i
gravi eccessi, vendicati sarem.

DONNA ANNA

Ma il padre, o Dio!

DON OTTAVIO

Convien chinare il ciglio ai volere del ciel. Respira, o cara.
Di tua perdita amara fia domani, se vuoi, dolce compenso
questo cor, questa mano, che il mio tenero amor.

DONNA ANNA

O dei, che dite in sì tristi momenti?

DON OTTAVIO

E che? Vorresti con indugi novelli accrescer le mie pene?
Crudele!

COMMENDATORE
    Yes!

DON GIOVANNI
    Bizarre, this situation:
    A corpse accepting my invitation.
    We must make preparation,
    So we'll be on our way.

LEPORELLO
    I'm getting palpitations
    I'm filled with agitation;
    For pity's sake let's hurry,
    I want to get away.

    [Exeunt.]

SCENE 12

[A dark room]

Recitative

DON OTTAVIO
    Do calm yourself, my darling; you soon will see that the
    criminal is caught and brought to justice; soon we'll have
    our revenge.

DONNA ANNA
    But my father, my father!

DON OTTAVIO
    We can only bow our heads to the will of the Lord. Take
    comfort, O dear one. I propose now to offer myself to
    replace the father you loved so – if you will, tomorrow,
    accept my hand and my heart.

DONNA ANNA
    Oh no! How can you? While I languish in mourning.

DON OTTAVIO
    But why persist in causing me such torment by postponing
    our marriage? You're heartless.

151

N. 23 Recitativo accompagnato e Rondo

DONNA ANNA

Crudele? Ah no, mio bene! Troppo mi spiace allontanarti un
ben che lungamente la nostr'alma desia. Ma il mondo, o
Dio! Non sedur la costanza del sensibil mio core; abbastanza
per te mi parla amore!

Non mi dir, bell'idol mio,
Che son io crudel con te.
Tu ben sai quant'io t'amai,
Tu conosci la mia fè.
Calma, calma il tuo tormento,
Se di duol non vuoi ch'io mora.
Forse un giorno il cielo ancora
Sentirà pietà di me.

[Parte.]

Recitativo

DON OTTAVIO

Ah, si segua il suo passo: io vo' con lei dividere i martiri:
saran meco men gravi i suoi sospiri.

[Parte.]

SCENA XIII

[sala in casa di Don Giovanni, con mensa preparata]

N. 24 Finale

DON GIOVANNI

Già la mensa è preparata.
Voi suonate, amici cari!
Giacchè spendo i miei danari,
Io mi voglio divertir.

Leporello, presto in tavola.

No. 23 Accompanied Recitative and Rondo

DONNA ANNA

I, heartless? Ah no, my dearest! I too regret my mourning must delay the happy moment when we become man and wife. But people . . . O heavens . . . Do not tempt me to abandon the solemn oath we swore together; for my heart will be yours now and forever.

Never say, my own beloved,
I could ever be cruel to you;
You've no reason to doubt I love you,
You know well my heart is true.
Calm, calm all your impatience
Or my grief will soon destroy me.
One day maybe heaven will hear me,
Hear my prayer and pity me.

[Exit.]

Recitative

DON OTTAVIO

Ah, I will follow her fortunes: I will go with her to share in all her sorrows; I must be at her side to ease all her tomorrows.

[Exit.]

SCENE 13

[Don Giovanni's dining hall, dinner laid]

No. 24 Finale

DON GIOVANNI

Now at last the table's ready.
You, my friends, let's hear you playing!
With the money I am paying
I expect to have my way.

Leporello, bring the pheasant in!

LEPORELLO
    Son prontissimo a servir.

    [Don Giovanni mangia; i suonatori cominciano a
    suonare.]

LEPORELLO
    Bravi! 'Cosa rara!'

DON GIOVANNI
    Che ti par del bel concerto?

LEPORELLO
    È conforme al vostro merto.

DON GIOVANNI
    Ah che piatto saporito!

LEPORELLO [a parte]
    Ah che barbaro appetito!
    Che bocconi da gigante!
    Mi par proprio di svenir.

DON GIOVANNI [a parte]
    Nel veder i miei bocconi,
    Gli par proprio di svenir.

    [A Leporello] Piatto!

LEPORELLO
    Servo!

    [I suonatori cominciano a suonare una tema da I Litiganti
    von Giuseppe Sarti.]

    Evvivano 'i litiganti.'

DON GIOVANNI
    Versa il vino!
    Eccellente marzimino!

LEPORELLO [a parte]
    Questo pezzo di fagiano,
    Piano piano, vo'inghiottir.

DON GIOVANNI [a parte]
    Sta mangiando, quel marrano!
    Fingerò di non capir.

LEPORELLO

Here it comes, without delay!

[He eats, and the orchestra begins to play.]

LEPORELLO

Bravi! 'Cosa rara'.

DON GIOVANNI

So you like this operetta?

LEPORELLO

The words are by da Ponte, but Mozart sets them better.[37]

DON GIOVANNI

Ah, this pheasant is delicious!

LEPORELLO *[aside]*

Ah, his appetite is vicious!
What enormous greedy mouthfuls!
I'm so hungry I feel faint.

DON GIOVANNI *[aside]*

He is watching while I'm eating
And he's looking rather faint.

[to Leporello] Next course!

LEPORELLO

Coming!

[The orchestra begins to play a theme from Sarti's 'I Litiganti'.]

That's still not as good as Mozart![38]

DON GIOVANNI

Pour the wine out.
What an excellent marzimino![39]

LEPORELLO *[aside]*

Here's the wishbone. We can't waste it.
If I quickly, quickly taste it, he won't see.

DON GIOVANNI *[aside]*

Look, the peasant eats my pheasant!
I'll pretend I did not see.

[I suonatori cominciano a suonare Non più andrai *da* Il Nozze di Figaro.]

LEPORELLO
Questa poi la conosco pur troppo.

DON GIOVANNI
Leporello!

LEPORELLO *[colla bocca piena]*
Padron mio!

DON GIOVANNI
Parla schietto, mascalzone.

LEPORELLO
Non mi lascia una flussione
Le parole proferir.

DON GIOVANNI
Mentre io mangio fischia un poco.

LEPORELLO
Non so far.

DON GIOVANNI
Cos'è?

LEPORELLO
Scusate, scusate!
Sì eccellente è il vostro cuoco,
Sì eccellente è il vostro cuoco,
Che lo volli anch'io provar.
Che lo volli anch'io provar.

DON GIOVANNI *[imitando Leporello]*
Sì eccellente è il cuoco mio,
Che lo volle anch'ei provar.

SCENA XIV

DONNA ELVIRA *[entra disperata]*
L'ultima prova dell'amor mio
Ancor vogl'io fare con te.

[The orchestra starts playing Non più andrai *from* The Marriage of Figaro]

LEPORELLO

There's a tune that is strangely familiar . . .

DON GIOVANNI

Leporello!

LEPORELLO *[with a mouthful]*

Just a moment!

DON GIOVANNI

Speak more clearly. I can't hear you!

LEPORELLO

I had better not come near you
As I seem to have a cold.

DON GIOVANNI

While I'm eating, whistle something.

LEPORELLO

Don't know how.

DON GIOVANNI

What's that?

LEPORELLO

Forgive me, forgive me,
Since your chef's so good with pheasant,
Such an artist with a pheasant,
Well, I thought it might be pleasant
Just to take a little bite.

DON GIOVANNI *[aping him]*

Since my chef is so good with pheasant,
Well, he thought he'd take a bite.

SCENE 14

DONNA ELVIRA *[entering, distraught]*

This is the last chance I'll ever offer:
You must fulfil your promise to me.

Più non rammento gl'inganni tuoi,
Pietade io sento.

DON GIOVANNI e LEPORELLO
Cos'è?

DONNA ELVIRA *[s'inginocchia]*
Da te non chiede quest'alma oppressa
Della sua fede qualche mercè.

DON GIOVANNI
Mi maraviglio! Cosa volete?
Se non sorgete non resto in piè.

[S'inginocchia.]

DONNA ELVIRA
Ah non deridere gli affanni miei!

LEPORELLO
Quasi da piangere mi fa costei.

DON GIOVANNI
Io ti deridere! Cieli, perchè?
Che vuoi, mio bene?

DONNA ELVIRA
Che vita cangi!

DON GIOVANNI
Brava!

DONNA ELVIRA
Cor perfido!

DON GIOVANNI
Lascia ch'io mangi,
E se ti piace,
Mangia con me.

DONNA ELVIRA
Restati, barbaro! Nel lezzo immondo
Esempio orribile d'iniquità!

LEPORELLO
Se non si muove del suo dolore,
Di sasso ha il core, o cor non ha.

I will forgive you all your transgressions.
I offer mercy.

DON GIOVANNI and LEPORELLO
  What for?

DONNA ELVIRA *[kneels]*
  Though you've abused me, I am now thinking
  Not of myself, but only of you.

DON GIOVANNI
  This is uncalled for. What are you asking?
  Well, if you must kneel, I will kneel too.

  [Kneels]

DONNA ELVIRA
  Ah, do not laugh at me when I am dying!

LEPORELLO
  My heart goes out to her; I feel like crying.

DON GIOVANNI *[mocking]*
  I would not laugh at you! Heavens! Not I!
  What are you asking?

DONNA ELVIRA
  For your repentance!

DON GIOVANNI
  Brava!

DONNA ELVIRA
  You'll never change!

DON GIOVANNI
  I'm eating dinner.
  Why don't you join me?
  Come and sit down.

DONNA ELVIRA
  Shameless philanderer! Back to your orgies!
  Rot in your cesspit of iniquity!

LEPORELLO
  If he's unmoved by her protestations,
  His heart is stone, if you ask me.

DON GIOVANNI
    Vivan le femmine,
    Viva il buon vino!
    Sostegno e gloria d'umanità!

    [Donna Elvira parte; grida]

DONNA ELVIRA
    Ah!

DON GIOVANNI e LEPORELLO
    Che grido è questo mai?

DON GIOVANNI
    Va' a veder che cosa è stato.

LEPORELLO *[sorte, e mette un grido]*
    Ah!

DON GIOVANNI
    Che grido indiavolato!

    [Leporello entra.]

    Leporello, che cos'è?

LEPORELLO
    Ah, signor! Per carità!
    Non andate fuor di qua!
    L'uom di sasso, l'uomo bianco,
    Ah padrone! Io gelo, io manco,
    Se vedeste che figura,
    Se sentiste come fa:
    Ta ta ta ta!

DON GIOVANNI
    Non capisco niente affatto.
    Tu sei matto in verità.

    [Qualcun batte alla porta]

LEPORELLO
    Ah sentite!

DON GIOVANNI
    Qualcun batte! Apri!

DON GIOVANNI
    I drink to women!
    I drink to wine![40]
    They are the reasons for being alive!

    [Donna Elvira, exiting, screams.]

DONNA ELVIRA
    Ah!

DON GIOVANNI and LEPORELLO
    What now? Why is she screaming?

DON GIOVANNI
    Go and see what is the matter.

LEPORELLO *[exits, screams.]*
    Ah!

DON GIOVANNI
    The devil must be out there!

    [Leporello returns.]

    Leporello, what is wrong?

LEPORELLO
    Ah, signor . . . where can I hide?
    Don't attempt to go outside.
    It's the marble statue walking . . .
    Through the darkness towards us he's stalking . . .
    If you saw his stony features,
    Heard the noise his footsteps make . . .
    Ta ta ta ta!

DON GIOVANNI
    Leporello, you've gone crazy!
    You've been drinking too much wine.

    [Someone knocks at the door.]

LEPORELLO
    Now d'you hear him?

DON GIOVANNI
    Someone's knocking. Open!

LEPORELLO

Io tremo!

DON GIOVANNI

Apri, dico!

LEPORELLO

Ah!

DON GIOVANNI

Matto! Per togliermi d'intrico
Ad aprir io stesso andrò.

LEPORELLO

Non vo' più veder l'amico,
Pian pianin m'asconderò.

[S'asconde sotto la tavola]

SCENA XV

COMMENDATORE

Don Giovanni, a cenar teco
M'invitasti, e son venuto!

DON GIOVANNI

Non l'avrei giammai creduto;
Ma farò quel che potrò.
Leporello, un altra cena
Fa che subito si porti!

LEPORELLO

Ah padron! Ah padron!
Ah padron, siam tutti morti.

DON GIOVANNI

Vanne dico!

COMMENDATORE

Ferma un po'!
Non si pasce di cibo mortale
Chi si pasce di cibo celeste!
Altre cure più gravi di queste,
Altra brama quaggiù mi guidò!

LEPORELLO

    I dare not.

DON GIOVANNI

    Open up, man!

LEPORELLO

    Ah!

DON GIOVANNI

    Idiot! If you are such a coward,
    I will have to go myself.

LEPORELLO

    I think underneath this table
    Is the place to go myself.

[He hides under the table. Enter the Commendatore's statue.]

SCENE 15

COMMENDATORE

    Don Giovanni, you kindly asked me
    Here to dinner, and I accepted.

DON GIOVANNI

    This is rather unexpected,
    But I'll do the best I can.
    Leporello, one more for dinner!
    Bring it quickly, lay the table!

LEPORELLO

    No, I can't, no, I can't.
    I am dead, so I'm unable.

DON GIOVANNI

    Go, obey me!

COMMENDATORE

    Stay where you are!
    One who's tasted the food of the angels
    Has no need for the diet of mortals.
    Other matters of much graver import,
    Other motives required me to come.

LEPORELLO

La terzana d'avere mi sembra,
E le membra fermar più non so.

DON GIOVANNI

Parla dunque! Che chiedi? Che vuoi?

COMMENDATORE

Parlo; ascolta! Più tempo non ho!

DON GIOVANNI

Parla, parla, ascoltando ti sto.

COMMENDATORE

Tu m'invitasti a cena,
Il tuo dover or sai.
Rispondimi, rispondimi,
Verrai tu a cenar meco?

LEPORELLO

Oibò! Tempo non ha, scusate.

DON GIOVANNI

A torto di viltate
Tacciato mai sarò.

COMMENDATORE

Risolvi!

DON GIOVANNI

Ho già risolto.

COMMENDATORE

Verrai?

LEPORELLO

Dite di no!

DON GIOVANNI

Ho fermo il core in petto.
Non ho timor: verrò!

COMMENDATORE

Dammi la mano in pegno!

DON GIOVANNI

Eccola! Ohimè!

LEPORELLO

I am in the last stages of dying.
I'm so scared that I shake like a leaf.

DON GIOVANNI

Please continue. What is it you're seeking?

COMMENDATORE

I speak, you listen. My time here is brief.

DON GIOVANNI

Speak then, speak. I am all disbelief.

COMMENDATORE

You asked me here to dinner.
Now I ask you, in my turn.
So answer me, so answer me:
Will you take dinner as my guest?

LEPORELLO

Oh no! He has a prior engagement.

DON GIOVANNI

I've never been a coward,
Nor will I be one now.

COMMENDATORE

Decide, then!

DON GIOVANNI

I have decided.

COMMENDATORE

You'll come, then?

LEPORELLO

You must say no!

DON GIOVANNI

I've told you I'm determined.
I'm not afraid: I'll go!

COMMENDATORE

Give me your hand to seal it.

DON GIOVANNI

Here it is. Ohimè!

COMMENDATORE

Cos'hai?

DON GIOVANNI

Che gelo è questo mai?

COMMENDATORE

Pentiti, cangia vita,
È l'ultimo momento!

DON GIOVANNI [vuol sciogliersi, ma invano]

No, no, ch'io non mi pento,
Vanne lontan da me!

COMMENDATORE

Pentiti, scellerato!

DON GIOVANNI

No, vecchio infatuato!

COMMENDATORE

Pentiti!

DON GIOVANNI

No!

COMMENDATORE

Sì!

DON GIOVANNI

No!

LEPORELLO

Sì, sì!

COMMENDATORE

Ah! tempo più non v'è!

[Fuoco da diverse parti; il Commendatore sparisce.
Terremoto.]

DON GIOVANNI

Da qual tremore insolito
Sento assalir gli spiriti!
Dond'escono quei vortici
Di foco pien d'orror?

COMMENDATORE
    Afraid?

DON GIOVANNI
    Your hand is deathly cold.

COMMENDATORE
    Your sins are black; repent them,
    Or face the flames of hellfire.

DON GIOVANNI *[trying, in vain, to free himself]*
    No, no, I'm not repentant.
    Go, get away from me!

COMMENDATORE
    Your sins are black; repent them.

DON GIOVANNI
    You fool! Why, you invent them.

COMMENDATORE
    Penitence!

DON GIOVANNI
    No!

COMMENDATORE
    Yes!

DON GIOVANNI
    No!

LEPORELLO
    Yes, yes!

COMMENDATORE
    Prepare to meet your doom!

    [The Commendatore disappears. The earth shakes, and flames leap up.]

DON GIOVANNI
    Terrors I've never known before
    Darken my spirit horribly.
    What are these swirling furnaces
    That scorch my soul with fear?

CORO DI SPETTRI [di sotterra, con voci cupe]
Tutto a tue colpe è poco!
Vieni, c'è un mal peggior!

DON GIOVANNI
Chi l'anima mi lacera?
Chi m'agita le viscere?
Che strazio, ohimè, che smania!
Che inferno, che terror!

LEPORELLO
Che ceffo disperato!
Che gesti da dannato!
Che gridi, che lamenti!
Come mi fa terror!

[Il fuoco cresce.]

DON GIOVANNI [resta inghiottito dalla terra]
Ah!

LEPORELLO
Ah!

SCENA ULTIMA

[Donna Anna, Donna Elvira, Zerlina, Don Ottavio,
Masetto, con ministri di giustizia]

DONNA ELVIRA, ZERLINA, DON OTTAVIO e MASETTO
Ah, dov'è il perfido?
Dov'è l'indegno?
Tutto il mio sdegno
Sfogar io vo'!

DONNA ANNA
Solo mirandolo
Stretto in catene
Alle mie pene
Calma darò.

LEPORELLO
Più non sperate
Di ritrovarlo,

CHORUS *[from beneath]*
> Well may you cry in anguish:
> Worse flames await you here.

DON GIOVANNI
> My soul is wracked with agony!
> My blood will boil in purgatory!
> What torment, ah, what torture!
> I'm burning! Death is near!

LEPORELLO
> What horrifying faces!
> The spasms of damnation!
> What screaming, what convulsions!
> I am consumed with fear.

> *[The flames increase.]*

DON GIOVANNI *[as the earth swallows him up]*
> Ah!

LEPORELLO
> Ah!

FINAL SCENE

[Enter Donna Anna, Donna Elvira, Zerlina, Don Ottavio, Masetto, with officers]

DONNA ELVIRA, ZERLINA, DON OTTAVIO and MASETTO
> Where is this infidel?
> Where is this villain?
> We seek revenge on
> Him and his kind.

DONNA ANNA
> Only the sight of him
> Chained here before me
> Could now restore me
> True peace of mind.

LEPORELLO
> In desperation
> Vainly you seek him.

Più non cercate,
Lontano andò.

DONNA ANNA, DONNA ELVIRA, ZERLINA, DON OTTAVIO e MASETTO
Cos'è! Favella!
Via, presto, sbrigati!

LEPORELLO
Venne un colosso . . .

DONNA ANNA, DONNA ELVIRA, ZERLINA, DON OTTAVIO e MASETTO
Via presto, sbrigati!

LEPORELLO
Ma se non posso!

DONNA ANNA, DONNA ELVIRA, ZERLINA, DON OTTAVIO e MASETTO
Presto, favella, sbrigati!

LEPORELLO
Tra fumo e foco
Badate un poco,
L'uomo di sasso,
Fermate il passo . . .
Giusto là sotto
Diede il gran botto,
Giusto là il diavolo
Se'l trangugiò!

DONNA ANNA, DONNA ELVIRA, ZERLINA, DON OTTAVIO e MASETTO
Stelle, che sento!

LEPORELLO
Vero è l'evento!

DONNA ELVIRA
Ah, certo è l'ombra
Che m'incontrò.

DONNA ANNA, ZERLINA, DON OTTAVIO e MASETTO
Ah, certo è l'ombra
Che l'incontrò.

His destination
You'll never find.

DONNA ANNA, DONNA ELVIRA, ZERLINA, DON OTTAVIO
and MASETTO

What's that? What happened?
Now, quickly, out with it!

LEPORELLO

There was this statue . . .

DONNA ANNA, DONNA ELVIRA, ZERLINA, DON OTTAVIO
and MASETTO

Now! Quickly! Out with it!

LEPORELLO

I cannot tell you!

DONNA ANNA, DONNA ELVIRA, ZERLINA, DON OTTAVIO
and MASETTO

Quickly, you tell us! Out with it!

LEPORELLO

Hellfire was smoking,
Had us both choking,
When Don Giovanni . . .
You won't believe me . . .
Shunned all repentance;
Heaven passed sentence;
Up came the devil and
Dragged him below.

DONNA ANNA, DONNA ELVIRA, ZERLINA, DON OTTAVIO
and MASETTO

You saw this happen?

LEPORELLO

I saw it happen.

DONNA ELVIRA

That was the phantom
I saw outside!

DONNA ANNA, ZERLINA, DON OTTAVIO and MASETTO

That was the phantom
She saw outside!

DON OTTAVIO

Or che tutti, o mio tesoro,
Vendicati siam dal cielo,
Porgi, porgi a me un ristoro,
Non mi far languire ancor.

DONNA ANNA

Lascia, o caro, un anno ancora
Allo sfogo del mio cor.

DON OTTAVIO e DONNA ANNA

Al desio di chi m'adora
Ceder deve un fido amor.

DONNA ELVIRA

Io men vado in un ritiro
A finir la vita mia!

ZERLINA e MASETTO

Noi, Masetto, a casa andiamo!
A cenar in compagnia!

LEPORELLO

Ed io vado all'osteria
A trovar padron miglior.

ZERLINA, LEPORELLO e MASETTO

Resti dunque quel birbon
Con Proserpina e Pluton.
E noi tutti, o buona gente,
Ripetiam allegramente
L'antichissima canzon.

TUTTI

Questo è il fin di chi fa mal;
E de' perfidi la morte
Alla vita è sempre ugual.

FINE DELL'OPERA

DON OTTAVIO

Now that heaven, my only treasure,
Has avenged us for your father,
Grant me, grant me this lasting pleasure,
Won't you let me make you my wife?

DONNA ANNA

Please allow me one year in mourning,
Then I'll prove my love for you.

DON OTTAVIO and DONNA ANNA

I will grant you all your wishes
As must lovers who are true.

DONNA ELVIRA

I'll withdraw into a convent,
There to seek my soul's salvation.

ZERLINA and MASETTO

Now our friends are all invited
To our wedding celebration.

LEPORELLO

If I go down to the tavern,
Will I find a better life?

ZERLINA, LEPORELLO and MASETTO

Don Giovanni's gone to dwell
With the devil down in hell.
So if you'd escape perdition,
We'll observe the old tradition
And an ancient moral tell.

ALL

Mend your ways, yes, mend them well.[41]
Mark the fate of Don Giovanni:
Sinners always burn in hell.

END

NOTES

Act 1.

1. *I must hide behind this door*
The literal translation here would be 'I don't want to be heard'. We wrote in the door to suit Philip Prowse's set for the ENO production, which consisted of three revolving towers offering varying vistas, exteriors and interiors, and several doorways. (See also Act 2 when Leporello is trying to escape from Elvira (130), and later in that scene, from Elvira, Zerlina, Masetto and Ottavio (130); in both these instances the 'porta' is in da Ponte.)

2. *Go back to bed, sir!*
Though this line (literally: 'It's beneath me / to fight with you') was invented for the rhyme, it conveys the characteristic insouciance with which the Don tackles a somewhat awkward situation.

3. *Oh God . . . swirling within my heart*
This was to prove one of the hardest passages in the whole piece to translate effectively. Our first version, which was influenced by Jonathan Miller's earliest ideas for the production ('Think,' he said, 'of *The Mysteries of Udolpho*') proved to be rather over-Gothic. In the event, ironically enough, this was the first moment where in performance, because of the busy orchestra and the allegro, alla breve tempo, it was well nigh impossible to hear the words anyway. But translators cannot permit themselves such thoughts. As often happened, after turning the phrase over in all our heads for days, the version that finally prevailed was virtually a literal translation of the original.

4. *And his eyes see round corners*
Again the set inspired this line (and the Don's three lines above, to which it responds), but it's a legitimate improvement on the literal 'And what eyesight!'

5. *You wormed your way into my house . . .*

In the Italian, Elvira moves into the historic present here. Da Ponte uses it again three times (Donna Anna 70, Leporello 76, and Don Giovanni 142) to add vividness to the narrative flow of the recitatives. In only the Anna and Giovanni examples, we felt, did the historic present work as well in contemporary English.

6. *A square is not a circle*

After poring over a dictionary of proverbs with us, Miller here preferred 'All cats are grey in the dark' (which, incidentally, turns up in Molière's *Barber of Seville*). We have opted for the more literal 'a square is not a circle', but it would be in the spirit of the moment to substitute any English proverb with a similar meaning.

7. *Little lady . . .*

The catalogue aria underwent several versions before everyone involved was finally happy. Again, we allowed Leporello some poetic licence in 'You're not going to like this', where the Italian says 'This is the list', but to underscore rather than undermine the theatrical moment.

8. *If she's blonde-haired . . .*

At the beginning of the (3/4) second half of the aria, there is a good example of Mozart's skill in setting a long phrase in Italian in several short two-bar sections. The motion of the music depends, partly, on the language being continuous, so it was essential to follow da Ponte's punctuation in our version.

9. *Like a mountain he will scale her*

'È la grande maestosa' is repeated in the original, but the temptation to retranslate the second line proved too great in this rare instance (see Introduction, p. 13). The rising scale in the music made the decision for us.

10. *Rich or poor, or wife or whore . . .*

Here, for the Italian 'picca, ricca, brutta, bella,' we substituted a quadruple rhyme. Da Ponte, we felt, might have approved, though our rhyme scheme follows the musical rather than the textual phrasing. As a general rule, at comic (or tragi-comic) moments like this, the rhymes came over so strongly in performance that we felt justified in allowing ourselves a little more freedom of movement away from the text.

11. *My Zerlina cannot stay here without me*

See note 22.

12. *I'll go drinking*

This departure from 'Resta, resta' ('You stay here, then') was forced by the need for a rhyme.

13. *These pretty hands for holding*

The Don literally says her hands feel 'like junket' (meaning they have not been hardened by housework) – an intriguing instance of how an 18th century peasant girl could be flattered.

14. *There will my arms enfold you*
The genesis of our version of 'Là ci darem la mano' is described in detail in the introduction.

15. *This clown is all I needed!*
'Intoppo' literally means obstacle or, more colloquially, the bung or cork put back in a half empty bottle. It proved an obstacle to us too. In colloquial Italian, the word is so rare an insult that it survives only in the Ricordi edition of the libretto; Barenreiter and Schirmer have 'Mancava questo in ver!' ('I certainly didn't need this!') 'Clown' catches the spirit of the word, if not quite its power, conveying Giovanni's dim view of Ottavio, with whom he was clearly acquainted before the action opens.

16. *my weapon . . . my power . . . I would spend, etc*
Apart from the Act 2 canzonetta, this is one of the most powerful examples of heavy sexual innuendo in the original Italian text, which we have tried to reproduce as tastefully as modern Opera House English permits.

17. *I know now!*
Donna Anna's invocation to 'O dei' ('Oh Gods'), repeated a semitone higher, leading to the final realisation on top A that it was Don Giovanni who murdered her father, sounds slightly quaint to our twentieth-century ears. In taking a liberty by substituting 'I know now!', we aspired to underline the immense tension of the moment, which is resolved on the top A 'He'.

18. *Silently he approaches me*
Historic present, as in the Italian. (See note 5 above: *You wormed your way into my house*).

19. *Her cares are my cares/Dalla sua pace*
Mozart added this lovely aria for the first Vienna production of the opera in 1788, a year after its première in Prague (see Introduction, page 19 and Appendix page 181).

20. *I took them home, Sir*
Historic present in the Italian. See note 5.

21. *First a flamenco*
Don Giovanni's first solo number is the mysteriously nicknamed 'Champagne' aria. In our efforts to reproduce the dances he asks Leporello to lay on, we managed to find three which were not merely authentically Spanish and eighteenth century, but whose names would mean something to a contemporary English audience.

22. *Your lovely little bride here . . .*
Don Giovanni, caught again trying to seduce Zerlina, taunts Masetto with virtually the same words ('La bella tua Zerlina non può, la

poverina, più star senza di te') as Masetto had used to Don Giovanni ('La Zerlina senza me non può star') at their first, ill-fated meeting. Our thanks to David Cairns for pointing this out.

23. *They won't be yours much longer . . .*
'He's set his heart on sin', to rhyme with 'my Lord invites you in', is a line which in performance always raised a laugh. This is excuse enough for the freedom of the translation, which would literally be 'Our friend will also try to make love to them.'

24. *Freedom for all, say I*
'Viva la libertà', the Don's famous laissez-faire slogan, was variously translated by Auden and Kallman: 'Do what you will is our only law / all that you may desire may here be done / do as thou wilt is here the law / thy will be done, thy will be done. Dent has 'I'm for a life that's gay, give me, give me a life that's gay', which might have made a better slogan for Auden and Kallman. Obviously the Dent version is unusable in the 1980s. Our repeatable 'Freedom for all, I say' fits both the Italian and the music accurately and uncontroversially enough.

25. *Retribution is at hand*
'Tutto, tutto già si sà' – literally, 'Everything, everything is now known'. We found it difficult to strengthen the sense of this sufficiently in English to match the growing menace of the Act I finale music. 'Retribution is at hand' seemed an acceptably sinister solution, forcing us to cry 'Vengeance' on the angry repeats of 'Tutto!' before a happily literal version of 'Trema, trema, scellerato!'

Act 2.

26. *You must be going blind*
Not in the original. Another liberty justified by the context, at the inexpensive price of losing 'caro il mio Leporello'.

27. *Ah, why this raging fever?*
Not, obviously, a literal translation of 'Ah taci, ingiusto core!' (Be still, my unfair heart!'). But literalism here would have involved distorting either words or music, so we opted for an alternative which seemed to echo the librettist's intentions.

28. *You have a heart of stone*
'Un' anima di bronzo' – literally, a soul of bronze (also presenting an impossible rhyme in the next line with 'gonzo'). This old English saying was, we felt, more than appropriate.

29. *She won't if you hide your face*
'Non ti conoscerà, se tu non vuoi' – literally, 'she won't recognise you if you don't want her to'. We found this adaptation, in the general

spirit of 'Not if you're careful', also helped theatrically in what is a highly visual scene.

30. *This should be fun to watch*
'Veggiamo che farà' – literally, 'Let's see what she does'. Another example of a line we felt entitled to embroider slightly in order to raise the required laugh.

31. *No, my Venus*
Leporello actually addresses Elvira as Venus seven lines further on, where it is musically impossible to make the name work in English. So we deliberately inserted it here, for 'muso bello', and for 'Mia Venere' substituted 'My Juliet' – Shakespeare's doomed heroine being one of the few legendary beauties (Eloise is another) whose name carries its stress on the first of three syllables.

32. *My Juliet*
See previous note.

33. *A suitor taking cover*
A deliberate alteration on our part of da Ponte's characteristically neat rhyme scheme. Because of the impossibility of rhyming 'Attack him!', the most effective English version of 'Ferite', which is the climactic word of the aria, we instead rhymed the last word of the previous line ('sentite') with our versions of 'ragazza' / 'piazza' ('lover / discover'). It did not seem to do too great a violence to da Ponte's intentions.

34. *Give him something to remember*
'Fracassargli le spalle' – literally, 'smash his shoulders'. As this hole-in-the-corner, Mafia-style beating up of peasant by nobleman is so powerfully set up by the text, we felt it appropriate here to substitute some colourful contemporary slang.

35. *He is my husband*
This is the only time Elvira so refers to Don Giovanni, presumably invoking (as in her recitative after 'Ah, chi me dice mai') his offer to marry her in Burgos, which we alas know from other scenes to be merely part of his standard seduction technique.

36. *This one is gorgeous . . .*
Historic present. See note 5 above: *You wormed your way into my house.*

37. *The words are by da Ponte, but Mozart sets them better* and
38. *That's still not as good as Mozart!*
See Introduction, page 21 for comment on this improvisation.

39. *Marzimino*
Much time was spent investigating this red Italian table wine to make sure it was an appropriate accompaniment to the Don's final pheasant. Our own investigations led us to an importers' warehouse in the London suburb of Kilburn, where we managed to track down a

case, only to discover that nowadays its taste is far from appropriate to its price.

40. *I drink to women! I drink to wine!*

This was the only moment outside the recitatives (see Introduction, page xx), where Mozart's exact notation had to be adjusted. The middle note of 'femmine' was omitted and the two crotchets on 'vino', a falling fifth, were changed to a minim on the lower note. Our musical colleagues agreed that this unusually drastic step was justified to make possible a literal and effective translation of the Don's final restatement of his credo.

41. *Mend your ways, yes, mend them well*

'Questo è il fin di chi fa mal' – literally, 'This is the end which befalls evildoers'. At the end of the opera's brief epilogue, coming as it does after the announcement of 'an ancient moral', we felt it more appropriate to sum up thus, reflecting the real sense of this first line in the two that follow.

APPENDIX

The following material, given here in a literal translation, was written for the first Vienna production in 1788. Mozart also wrote Don Ottavio's aria 'Dalla Sua Pace' (Act 1, page 74) as a substitute for his aria 'Il Mio Tesoro' (Act 2, page 138), and the Recitative and Aria for Donna Elvira 'In quali eccessi/Mi tradi' (Act 2, page 138), for this production. We have included them in the main text as they are so often performed.

Apart from those two arias the Vienna version material consists of these extra scenes between Leporello, Zerlina, the silent contadino, Masetto and Donna Elvira. They are not usually considered worthy of inclusion, being both dramatically and musically weak, despite the bright C major charm of the duet 'Per queste tue manine' for Leporello and Zerlina.

The whole section belongs after Masetto's 'Accoppatelo meco tutti tre' (page 134). Leporello's aria 'Ah Pieta Signori Miei!' (page 134) was also omitted in Vienna.

The hybrid version often used (at ENO and elsewhere) adds the 'Mi Tradi' scene written for Vienna to the original Prague version of 1787. The slightly unsatisfactory result is the sheer length of the three arias 'Il mio tesoro', 'Mi tradi' and, after the graveyard scene, 'Non mi dir', which collectively slow the action of the opera at the heart of its second act.

In our view 'Dalla sua pace', however, comes at a point in Act 1 where its inclusion follows quite logically from Don Ottavio's recitative. Others believe it over-balances the drama at this crucial early stage too much towards the relatively peripheral figure of Ottavio.

ATTO SECONDO, in Scena 9

Recitativo

LEPORELLO
Ah pietà . . . compassion . . . misericordia!

DON OTTAVIO
Non lo sperar!

LEPORELLO
Udite . . . in questo loco . . . era aperta la porta . . . Don Giovanni pose a me questi panni, ed io con lei . . . scusate, io non ci ho colpa . . . In quel momento capitaste coi servi . . . Il lume fuggo . . . sbaglio le stanze . . . giro . . . giro . . . giro . . . mi schermisco . . . m'intoppo. In altri incontro . . . di là mi volgo, mi caccio qua, ma s'io sapeva fuggia per là!

SCENA 10a

[Zerlina con coltello alla mano conduce fuori Leporello per i capelli]

ZERLINA
Restati qua!

LEPORELLO
Per carità! Zerlina!

ZERLINA
Eh, non c'è carità pei pari tuoi!

LEPORELLO
Dunque cavarmi vuoi . . .

ZERLINA
. . . i capelli, la testa, il core e gli occhi.

LEPORELLO *[vuol farle alcune smorfie]*
Senti, carina mia . . .

ACT TWO, in Scene 9

Recitative

LEPORELLO

Ah, have pity . . . compassion . . . mercy!

DON OTTAVIO

There's no hope for you!

LEPORELLO

Listen . . . in this place . . . the door was open . . . Don Giovanni insisted that I wear these clothes . . . and I did . . . excuse me, it isn't my fault . . . At that moment, when you arrived with the servants . . . I fled from the light . . . not realising where I was . . . I tried this way . . . and that . . . defending myself . . . then stumbled. I met others, and turning away, I ended up here: but if I had known I would have escaped this way!

SCENE 10a

[Zerlina, with a knife in her hand, drags Leporello in by his hair.]

ZERLINA

Stay there!

LEPORELLO

For pity's sake, Zerlina!

ZERLINA

Eh! There'll be no pity for the likes of you.

LEPORELLO

Then you intend to tear out . . .

ZERLINA

. . . your hair, head, heart and eyes!

LEPORELLO *[trying to flatter her]*

Listen, my dear.

ZERLINA

Guai se mi tocchi! Vedrai schiuma de' birbi, qual premio n'ha chi le ragazze ingiuiria.

LEPORELLO *[a parte]*

Liberatemi, o Dei, da questa furia!

ZERLINA *[si strascina dietro per tutta la scena Leporello]*

Masetto . . . olà! Masetto! Dove diavolo è ito . . . servi . . . gente . . . nessun vien . . . nessun sente . . .

LEPORELLO

Fa' piano per pietà . . . non strascinarmi a coda di cavallo!

ZERLINA

Vedrai come finisce il ballo. Presto qua quella sedia.

LEPORELLO

Eccola.

ZERLINA

Siedi.

LEPORELLO

Stanco non son!

ZERLINA

Siedi, o con queste mani ti strappo il cor, e poi lo getto a' cani.

LEPORELLO

Siedo: ma tu, di grazia, metti giù quel rasoio. Mi vuoi forse sbarbar?

ZERLINA

Sì, mascalzone! io sbarbare ti vo' senza sapone.

LEPORELLO

Eterni Dei!

ZERLINA

Dammi la man!

LEPORELLO *[esita]*

La mano.

ZERLINA

There'll be trouble if you touch me. You'll see, you scum of the earth, what happens to a man who insults girls.

LEPORELLO *[aside]*

Ye Gods, free me from this Fury!

ZERLINA *[calling across the stage, dragging Leporello behind her]*

Masetto . . . hey there, Masetto! Where the devil has he gone . . . servants . . . people . . . no one comes . . . no one hears . . .

LEPORELLO

Be quiet, for pity's sake. Don't drag me about like a horse by the tail.

ZERLINA

You'll see how the party will end. Quick, pass me that chair.

LEPORELLO

Here you are.

ZERLINA

Sit down.

LEPORELLO

I'm not tired.

ZERLINA *[pulling a razor from her pocket]*

Sit down, or I'll rip out your heart with my bare hands, and then throw it to the dogs.

LEPORELLO

I'll sit, but for God's sake put that razor away. Or do you want to shave me?

ZERLINA

Yes, you rogue, I want to shave you without soap.

LEPORELLO

Eternal Gods!

ZERLINA

Give me your hand!

LEPORELLO *[hesitating]*

My hand?

ZERLINA [*minacciandolo*]
    L'altra!

LEPORELLO
    Ma che vuoi farmi?

ZERLINA
    Voglio far quello che parmi.

    [*Zerlina lega le mani a Leporello col fazzoletto.*]

N. 21a Duetto

LEPORELLO
    Per queste tue manine candide e tenerelle,
    Per questa fresca pelle, abbi pietà di me!

ZERLINA
    Non v'è pietà, briccone, son una tigre irata,
    Un aspide, un leone, no, pietà non v'è!

LEPORELLO
    Ah di fuggir si provi!

ZERLINA
    Sei morto se ti muovi!

LEPORELLO
    Barbari, ingiusti Dei!

ZERLINA [*lo lega con una corda sulla sedia*]
    Barbaro traditore!
    Del tuo padrone il core avessi qui con te!

LEPORELLO
    In mano di costei chi capitar mi fe'!
    Deh non mi stringer tanto! L'anima mia sen va.

ZERLINA
    Sen vada o resti, intanto non partirai di qua.

LEPORELLO
    Che strette . . . oh Dei, che botte!
    È giorno, ovver . . . è notte?

ZERLINA
    Di gioia e di diletto sento brillarmi il petto. Così, così
    cogl'uomini, così, così si fa. Sei morto se ti muovi!

ZERLINA *[menacingly]*

Now the other.

LEPORELLO

But what are you going to do to me?

ZERLINA

I'll do whatever I feel like doing.

[Zerlina ties Leporello's hands with a handkerchief.]

No. 21a Duet

LEPORELLO

By these your hands, white and soft,
By this white skin, have pity on me!

ZERLINA

There'll be no pity, villain. I'm an angry tiger,
An asp, a lion. No, I've no pity!

LEPORELLO

Ah, if only I could try to escape!

ZERLINA

If you move, you're a dead man!

LEPORELLO

Barbarous, unjust Gods!

ZERLINA *[as she ties him to the chair with a rope]*

Barbarous traitor!
If only you had your master's heart here with you!

LEPORELLO

How did I fall into the hands of this woman?
God, don't pull so tight! I can't breathe.

ZERLINA

Dead or alive, you aren't going to leave this place.

LEPORELLO

What squeezing, oh God what blows!
Is it day or night?

ZERLINA

I feel my breast rejoicing with joy and pleasure! This is the
way to handle men. You're dead if you move!

LEPORELLO
Che scosse . . . di . . . tremuoto!
Che buia oscurità!
Ah di fuggir si provi!

SCENA 10b

Recitativo

LEPORELLO *[seduto e legato, ad un contadino che passa in fondo della scena]*
Amico, per pietà, un poco d'acqua fresca, o ch'io mi moro. Guarda un po'come stretto mi legò l'assassina! Se potessi liberarmi coi denti! Oh venga il diavolo a disfar questi gruppi! Io vo'vedere di rompere la corda . . . Come è forte . . . Paura della morte! E tu, Mercurio, protettor de' ladri, proteggi un galantuom . . . Coraggio . . . bravo! . . . Ciel, che veggio! . . . Non serve; pria che costei ritorni bisogna dar di sprone alla calcagna e strascinar, se occorre una montagna.

[Tira forte, cade la finestra ove sta legato il capo della corda; fugge strascinando seco sedia e porta.]

SCENA 10c

Recitativo

ZERLINA
Andiam signora, vedrete in qual maniera ho concio il scellerato.

DONNA ELVIRA
Ah sopra lui si sfoghi il mio furor!

ZERLINA
Stelle! in qual modo si salvò quel briccon?

MASETTO
No, non si trova un' anima più nera.

LEPORELLO
What tremors . . . of . . . earthquake!
What black darkness!
Ah, if only I could try to escape!

SCENE 10b

Recitative

LEPORELLO *[seated and tied up, speaking to a peasant who is passing by]*
Friend, for pity's sake, give me a drop of water, or I'll die! Look here, how tightly that murderess has tied me! If only I could free myself with my teeth! Oh, would that the devil could come and untie these knots! I want to see if I can break the rope . . . how strong it is! Oh, fear of death! And you, Mercury, protector of thieves, protect an honest man! Courage! Bravo! Heavens, what do I see! . . . He won't help; before that woman comes back, I must take to my heels – and drag a mountain with me, if I have to.

[He pulls hard; the window, to which the end of the rope is tied, falls out.]

SCENE 10c

Recitative

ZERLINA
Come, Signora, you will see how I have caught the villain.

DONNA ELVIRA
Ah, I will vent all my fury on him!

ZERLINA
Heavens! How on earth has that wretch saved himself?

MASETTO
You'll never find a blacker soul.

ZERLINA

Ah, Masetto, dove fosti finor?

MASETTO

Un' infelice volle il ciel ch'io salvassi. Era io sol pochi passi lontan da te, qualdo gridare io sento nell'opposto sentiero: con lor v'accorro; veggio una donna che pianga, ed un uomo che fugge: vo'inseguirlo, mi sparisce dagli occhi, ma da quel che mi disse la fanciulla, ai tratti, alle sembianze, alle maniere lo credo quel briccon del cavaliere.

ZERLINA

È desso senza fallo: anche di questo informiam Don Ottavio: a lui si aspetta far per noi tutti, o domandar vendetta.

ZERLINA

Ah, Masetto, where have you been all this time?

MASETTO

Heaven willed that I save an unfortunate one. I was only a few paces away from you when I heard cries coming from the path over there: I rushed over; I saw a lady crying, and a man running away: I followed him, but he vanished before my very eyes, but from what the lady told me about him, his looks and his behaviour exactly match those of that villain of a gentleman.

ZERLINA

It must have been him. I will tell Don Ottavio about this too; it is up to him to act for all of us, or to ask for vengeance.